PRAISE FOR

The Smart Girl's Guide to Privacy

"An illuminating handbook for women."
—ELLE MAGAZINE

"A must-read . . . addressing not only the why of keeping strong boundaries but the how."
—FOREWORD REVIEWS

"Violet Blue is not just a writer and journalist; she's also a friend and advocate to every female who has a computer or smart phone. . . . Highly recommended for public and school libraries, as well as social science and technology classes."
—BECKY WALTON, INGRAM COLLECTION DEVELOPMENT LIBRARIAN

"Alarmingly handy . . . a straightforward how-to for protecting your privacy and undermining the social media settings that want you to share intimate details with the world."
—BITCH MAGAZINE

"A must-read for anyone who uses their laptop or phone to go online."
—DAME MAGAZINE

the smart girl's guide to privacy

practical tips for staying safe online

violet blue

no starch press

Printed in USA

Second printing

19 18 17 16 15   2 3 4 5 6 7 8 9

SUSTAINABLE FORESTRY INITIATIVE   Certified Sourcing   www.sfiprogram.org   SFI-00854

Text stock is SFI certified

ISBN-10: 1-59327-648-6
ISBN-13: 978-1-59327-648-5

Publisher: William Pollock
Production Editor: Laurel Chun
Cover and Interior Design: Beth Middleworth
Developmental Editors: William Pollock and Jennifer Griffith-Delgado
Compositor: Laurel Chun
Proofreader: Lisa Devoto Farrell
Indexer: BIM Indexing & Proofreading Services

For information on distribution, translations, or bulk sales,
please contact No Starch Press, Inc. directly:

No Starch Press, Inc.
245 8th Street, San Francisco, CA 94103
phone: 415.863.9900; info@nostarch.com
www.nostarch.com

Library of Congress Cataloging-in-Publication Data

Blue, Violet.
  The smart girl's guide to privacy : practical tips for staying safe online / by Violet Blue.
    pages cm
  Summary: "Discusses how to protect personal information from online privacy violations. Covers how to set and store secure passwords, monitor online visibility, safely use social media and apps, and create online profiles. Contains emergency instructions for those who have been hacked or had their identity, phone, or laptop stolen"-- Provided by publisher.
  ISBN 978-1-59327-648-5 -- ISBN 1-59327-648-6
  1. Computer crimes--Prevention. 2. Internet--Security measures. 3. Internet and women. 4. Internet--Safety measures. 5. Privacy, Right of. I. Title.
  HV6773.B56 2015
  613.6'602854678--dc23
                                        2015013420

brief contents

contents in detail

3
you got hacked   31

4
female trouble   49

5
identity theft 69

6
how to share 81

7
people-search websites

8
dating and sexytime

9
ninja tricks

10
I hate passwords   133

resources   141

index   155

"At one point I thought changing my name might help with privacy, but that was before the Internet." —Olivia Wilde

1. get smart

Social media, online dating, photo sharing, mobile apps, and more can make a modern girl's social life a dream—or a nightmare. When you just want to feel connected to friends, family, and romance, the last things you want to deal with are potential dangers like identity theft, online stalking, corporate information sharing, or revenge porn. For many women, getting control of their online privacy is confusing, overwhelming, and stressful.

This book is packed with some serious self-defense moves. It's designed to help you get organized so you can navigate the chaotic landscape of online privacy. In these pages you'll find a guide to making sure you don't share too much. You'll learn how to look good to potential employers (or potential dates) and safeguard your privacy from sleazy marketers, unethical megacorporations, scammers, stalkers, bullshit artists, and anyone who wants to silence women online. And it does all this without making you feel judged, paranoid, or like a total newbie.

Traditionally, women haven't been taught to stand up for themselves the way men have—whether online or anyplace else—but this is changing. Today, women are standing up to stalkers and being more careful than ever with personal information. We're getting fierce, angry, and strategic. We don't have time for shame, and the haters are losing. These are significant signs of much-needed changes in women's roles, especially in our role as consumers.

One of the major obstacles we face in protecting ourselves is that most social media websites are not designed to safeguard people who are targets. While there are a lot of amazing female programmers and powerful women working in the security and technology sectors, most sites and social sharing apps are designed by men who don't take into account that half the users will experience particular kinds of predatory behavior. Thus, the rules and structures of these online tools permit them to be used for evil.

In addition, the tech industry is full of corporate greed and douchebags and a whole lot of bad security practices. Most online services, such as bill-paying websites, and mobile apps are made shoddily and leak private information like there's no tomorrow. It's enough to make you wonder why every person you know hasn't had their identity stolen yet.

Privacy can be something you want just to feel safe, or you may have read horror stories about things happening to other women (maybe even your friends) and want to make sure that those things never happen to you. Maybe you're interested in being downright badass about your privacy because you've had a bad experience—or maybe you're dealing with a privacy or reputation crisis right now.

No matter what brought you to these pages, this book will give you control and power over something that would otherwise have the power to hurt you and the people you love. And if you're reading this because you've lost control, there's good news: you're about to get your power back.

In the first two chapters, you'll find a lot of suggestions that will help you define what you want to keep private and what you're okay with sharing. Be prepared to take a few missteps as you get started—there will be a bit of a learning curve—but know that I'll give you the basics to keep what matters, like your home address, from getting into the wrong hands. Once you nail down your boundaries, determine who puts you at risk and what the risks are, and identify the bad guys, your life will feel more like an adventure from a place of freedom and power than a disaster waiting to happen.

Speaking of disasters, it's not just provocative or racy photos that can get stolen and ridiculed (or worse) to hurt you online. You don't need to be a flirt to get singled out. For someone who decides to target you, your presence is enough—if you don't protect yourself. When you protect yourself, however, you actually can post or share sexy pictures of yourself and stay in control. The key is knowing what to protect, knowing what sites and apps you can (and can't) trust, and removing from view anything that can compromise you.

You can start taking control of your private information right now. Find out what information is out there about you by searching for yourself. Searching for yourself might be daunting, even scary, and it might bring up negative feelings, but this is where you start getting tough on controlling your private property. Knowing is always better—and safer—than not knowing.

TAKE THE ONLINE PRIVACY TEST

The first step to taking control is a privacy check-up. Follow these instructions now, and don't panic if you find something online you didn't expect:

- Google your name using quotation marks, like "Anna Jones" (and be sure to check the Images tab).

- Google your phone number.

- Google your home address.

- Google your Social Security number (tax ID).

- Do a Google reverse image search of your most-recently shared photos.

- Search your own name on Spokeo, USSearch, or Intelius.

Don't blame yourself for what companies like Facebook, LinkedIn, Google, online advertising companies, and data brokers have done to your privacy. And don't panic if you see something you didn't realize was public: what's online doesn't have to stay visible forever. Along with how to prevent a privacy disaster, this book will show you how to fix some of the worst things you'll find about yourself online.

EIGHT PRIVACY TIPS TO USE RIGHT NOW

Every three months, do a privacy check-up that includes searching for your name, phone number, and address, as well as online accounts such as Facebook, Twitter, Google, and your bank. But you can take some actions immediately to make yourself safer online and, hopefully, improve what you see in those check-ups.

1. Use different email addresses for different online accounts. You can set them up to forward email to the address you actually check.

2. View your Facebook, LinkedIn, and Google+ profiles as someone else, and then adjust the privacy settings.

3. Tape over your webcam.

4. Activate the password lock on your phone, laptop, and tablet.

5. Never sign in on someone else's phone, computer, or tablet.

6. Look into getting a free, Internet-based VoIP (Voice over Internet Protocol) phone number to use for any online communications. Don't worry—you can forward it.

7. Consider getting a post office box that you can use in place of your home address to minimize the risk of identity theft, stalking, and other dangers.

8. Install two or three antitracking plug-ins and extensions in your browser, such as AdBlock Plus, Disconnect, Abine's Blur, or Ghostery.

If you want to be extra vigilant or if you have known enemies online, you can also set up a Google Custom Alert at *http://google.com/alerts/*. When you do, you'll get an email notification whenever your name, email address, or phone number is added to Google's searched sites. Note that Google Alerts sends you only the *newly* indexed results for your search since the last time it checked, not every result there is. You can set up as many alerts as you like, and enter multiple words for each search. Try to use specific search terms so you don't end up with frustratingly general results. To search for an exact phrase, put quotes around your words (like "Anna Jones"), and finish up by selecting the areas you want Google to cover (News, Blogs, and so on) and how often you want the results delivered. Once you're done, bookmark the Google Alerts page so you can go back and manage your Alerts or edit them to work better for you.

TARGETS AND NONTARGETS

Google's Eric Schmidt said, "If you have something you don't want anyone to know, maybe you shouldn't be doing it in the first place."* Actor and tech investor Ashton Kutcher and Facebook's Mark Zuckerberg have each said that if you're not doing anything "wrong," then you don't have anything to worry about when it comes to losing your privacy. That's easy—and profitable—for them to say. They make money on getting you to give up as many details about your life as they can grab.

Why, exactly, does Ashton Kutcher get to decide that whatever you're doing is wrong just because you don't want the whole world to know about it? Filthy-rich celebrities are more able than the rest of us to hide things they consider private or embarrassing because they can afford to. Wanting to keep something private doesn't mean you did anything wrong, and you shouldn't feel ashamed for protecting your privacy. These people are trafficking in beliefs from a bygone era, like laughably antiquated notions about female hysteria and women having to choose between a job and a family.

The most important problem with modern privacy discussions is that we aren't addressing the critical difference between how men and women perceive privacy—most men aren't targets, but most women are. When the agenda of privacy discussions is set by men like Schmidt, Kutcher, and Zuckerberg, they sound completely crazy and disconnected from reality. They don't understand what we experience every day as targets. This lack of understanding manifests in these decision-makers' attitudes about privacy and safety, as well as decisions about user experience design and implementation that put those who bear target status—namely, women—at even greater risk than those who don't.

---

* Eric Schmidt, interview by Maria Bartiromo, CNBC, December 3, 2009, retrieved from *http://www.huffingtonpost.com/2009/12/07/google-ceo-on-privacy-if_n_383105.html.*

If you've never gone online as a guy, try it. Use a male name next time you make a throwaway account on Reddit or other social media sites. Being male online will blow your mind. You'll never fully appreciate what it's like not to be targeted and just how differently you will be treated by groups, businesses, and other individuals until you spend time online as a man.

As women, we're targeted just because we show up. Every time we go on Facebook or leave a comment with a female name attached to it, we're checked out for sex, we're judged accordingly, and the nontargets act on their judgment. Nonetheless, many young women aren't even aware that they bear target status.

Most guys don't think about what it's like to be sized up for sexual value as the first thing anyone sees about them, everywhere they go—anytime they go online, walk into a room, or try to join a conversation. Most men don't have to deal with being a target their whole lives the same way that women do—including people who are female gendered, female-bodied, and all along the spectrum of gender expression.

Men also feel more comfortable drawing attention to themselves when they feel targeted than women do. Guys are often louder when they've been targeted, whereas women have become trained to be lone soldiers online, knowing that to send up a signal flare for help is more likely to attract enemies than allies.

The privacy settings at social media sites and apps have a baseline of normal that doesn't consider the fact that half of their users are being targeted. The situation sucks, because in fact we have a lot of male allies out there. This book and the many conversations women are having about these issues are raising the profile of target status. Soon, ignorance will be no defense.

This book is for women of all ages, and I'd be remiss not to say that it's also for women of all shades on the gender identity spectrum and that people of all genders and orientations are warmly welcomed here. Females aren't the only ones who bear target status. Women attack and stalk, too, and LGBTQ people are routinely left out of the privacy conversation—or worse, ignored altogether.

LOSING YOUR PRIVACY

Some people might try to tell you that by being online, sharing photos, or having a public presence on the Internet, you're somehow "asking for it." Don't fall for this. Just because a girl wears a skirt, is she "asking for" sexual assault? Of course not. People make these arguments when you're not giving them what they want—and what they want is something private from you. When you refuse to give these people what they want by standing your ground about something private, they often get mean and angry. The idea that consumers somehow deserve to be violated because we want to live our lives on our own terms is a hurtful myth that's used to make us feel ashamed so we won't stand up for ourselves.

Privacy is your right. Assuming you're not an ax murderer, it's up to you to decide what you want to keep private, and whatever you want to keep private is worth protecting. Don't let anyone—no matter how important, famous, or powerful— make you feel ashamed about standing up for your boundaries. Only those who have proven that they'll treat your personal stuff responsibly should get access to it, and the only one who can truly protect your privacy is you.

When you lose your privacy, personal things are shared with strangers that

- are embarrassing;
- are hurtful;
- put you in danger;

- may cause you to lose things you care about or need, like money, child custody, or employment;

- may cause you to lose your job or get kicked out of school (or hurt your chances of getting a job, and so on);

- ruin your reputation;

- are used to tell lies about you;

- expose the privacy of people you care about (such as your family members), putting them at risk; and

- make it easy for criminals to steal your identity.

The loss of your private information can affect your family, employment, education, relationships, credit, online memories, mental and emotional health, friends, and reputation. Having your private information fall into the hands of stalkers, data brokers, competitors, exes, anyone who is mad at you, people who think it's fun to hurt random strangers, and companies that profit from selling information to advertisers or other shoppers can ruin your life.

Ways You Can Lose Your Privacy

You can lose your privacy in a number of ways, and most of the time, it's not your fault. Often, your privacy gets violated because no one warned you about what to look out for or who not to trust. The ways your privacy gets screwed with—privacy threats—fall into four categories.

PEOPLE WITH GOOD INTENTIONS

- Friends sharing your location, like with check-ins

- People taking photos or video of you without your permission

- Someone accidentally (or intentionally) seeing your computer, phone, or tablet screen while you log in, sign up for something, make a purchase, or open an application such as iPhoto

PEOPLE WITH EVIL INTENTIONS

- Someone sharing personal or sexual photos (or videos) without your consent

- Hackers or creeps spying through your webcams

- Someone making embarrassing information public or sending private details about you to people like your boss

- Malicious people publishing your private information (like your address) online

GREEDY, DOUCHEY COMPANIES

- Websites changing settings and making private things public

- Websites tricking you into entering personal information

- Companies like online stores, Google, Facebook and other social media sites, email services, and others selling your personal information to other companies (like their advertisers or third-party affiliates)

- People-finder services buying and collecting your private information and making it available for purchase

OOPS . . . ACCIDENTS

- Not realizing that something you put online is public

- Not knowing which things to avoid sharing online

- Not using a password on your phone, laptop, certain apps, or file folders

- Unclear website privacy settings causing you to make private things public

PROTECT YOURSELF RIGHT NOW

With so many ways your privacy can be compromised, it can seem like being safe is at odds with having a life online—especially if you intend to be at all sexy or sexual. But you don't have to live a boring, antisocial life to be safe. You can protect yourself.

Some people feel like they can't do anything online without putting themselves at risk. But being online and using social media, different apps, photo-sharing websites, or even dating sites can be as safe as you want it to be. When you get in a car, you put on your seat belt. When you get on a motorcycle, you put on a helmet. When you get on the Internet, it's as safe as you make it. Here are some things to do right now.

Tape Over Your Webcam

Everything has a camera. Your phone, your laptop, your tablet, your Kindle. If you have a modern device that can get online, it probably has a camera. And if it has a camera, someone looking for cash or scummy thrills has figured out how to hack into it and turn it on without triggering the *on* light. No joke. That's why you need to put a piece of tape over your webcam, even when it's off or if you never use it.

A year before Cassidy Wolf was crowned Miss Teen USA 2013, a guy in her high school used a program to hack into the webcam on her computer and take photos of her. She found out when he got into her social media accounts and tried to extort money from her. It turns out that she was one of 12 girls he had taken photos of and threatened for cash. You can bet he shared the photos; there are forums where guys who run these cam scams post photos they collect. Don't believe me? Google "ex-girlfriend pictures" or type it into any torrent search engine.

You can make your camera worthless for spying—but still usable when you choose—by keeping it taped up. Sticky notes work well because they have a gentle adhesive and are easy to replace. You can also find privacy stickers for purchase online that are made specifically for putting on (and taking off) web and phone cameras.

Cassidy Wolf's malicious hacker used a program that turned on cameras without activating the light or doing anything to let the girls know they were being spied on. In fact, this happens more often than it gets reported in the news.

There's a huge black market for compromised webcams and the video or photos they can record, and unsurprisingly, cams belonging to girls and the images that can be stolen from them are worth the most amount of money. Such programs are typically put on a computer when the victim clicks a link, often through an email, and they infect the computer with a program that hides while letting the computer's camera be controlled remotely. This is just one form of an online hack attack called *phishing*. (Learn more about phishing, how to spot it, and how to avoid becoming a phishing victim in Chapter 5, "Identity Theft.")

After her harrowing experience, Ms. Wolf now tapes over all of her webcams, changes her passwords, never uses someone else's computer or phone, and never reveals personal details to strangers or "friends" she just met. That's what you should be doing, too.

Lock Your Phone, Computer, and Tablet

Put a password or personal identification number (PIN) on your computer, tablet, and phone. There's a Creepy Steve in every café, on every bus, in your friend circle, and among your family's friends. If Creepy Steve sits down at your computer or picks up your phone, iPad, or Kindle when you go pee, and you didn't lock it, he's got access to any account you left open. This can include email, messaging and chat, social media, photographs, personal files, Internet history, and even bank accounts.

It's even scarier when your device has been stolen, because the attacker has all the time in the world (or at least until you notice the theft) to rummage through your accounts. (If you hate passwords and PINs annoy you and slow everything down, don't miss Chapter 10, "I Hate Passwords.")

Do a Privacy Check-Up

Make a list of your online accounts and apps and set aside one hour to double-check your privacy settings. If it sounds as fun as doing household chores, that's because it is. Unfortunately, sites like Facebook like to screw with your privacy settings, so chances are good that if you haven't checked your settings in the past few months, you might be revealing something you will regret.

You'll worry less about the privacy bait and switch these sites like to play on users after you read Chapter 6, "How to Share." For now, just bite the bullet, do a privacy check-up, and reward yourself afterward because you're worth it. You'll feel 1,000 percent better when it's done, I promise.

Don't Email Your ID

Never scan or photograph your ID and send it to anyone online—even to Google or Facebook. No one should be asking for your ID, and you're not legally required to show it. Companies that ask are treading a thin line, and you have no way of knowing if the information you share is really, definitely safe. ID information could hand an identity thief the keys to your entire life. (When you read about identity theft and how to avoid or fix it in Chapter 5, you'll see why you shouldn't send your ID via email, text, or any other unsecured way online.)

Many people-finder websites (also called "people search" or "people lookup" services) require that you scan and provide your ID in order to opt out of them selling your information. They even have onerous procedures such as accepting opt-out request letters only via fax or postal mail. This seems to be standard practice. To stay safe, never scan and send your ID to anyone without blacking out your photo and ID number. Find out more in Chapter 7, "People-Search Websites."

Use a Password Manager and Install an Antitheft App

Don't ever let your computer or your browser save (or "remember") your passwords. Use a password manager like 1Password, LastPass, KeePass, or any of the recommendations in the Resources section.

Along with a password manager, install an antitheft app like Prey or Lookout. You can download these apps to your computer or phone, giving you the power to track your devices if they get stolen or used by someone else.

Antitheft apps can camouflage themselves as games and lock and remotely wipe your devices. They can show you where your device is on a map, take photos from the device's camera, and upload those photos to your online account. You'll be able to see not only where your laptop or phone is but also who has it, and you can give this information to the police. These apps all do things a little differently, but the general idea is the same.

BE THE FIREWALL

Remember that *you* decide what information about yourself to reveal and when, why, and to whom. Social tech empowers you to run your own social life, but it can just as easily put you in the crosshairs of stalkers and criminals. Sometimes it feels like protecting your privacy is a full-time job, with more-than-occasional midnight and weekend shifts for good measure.

This book changes all of that. In the following chapters, you'll find answers to help you conquer every privacy puzzle, including how to have revenge porn taken down, remove your information from people-search sites, survive having your identity stolen, date safely, conquer the insanity of social media privacy, and much more.

The best part is that you don't have to give up doing anything you like. Don't worry if you can't do every single thing in this book. Even taking just four actions from the "Eight Privacy Tips to Use Right Now" on page 4 will tip the privacy scales in your favor.

From now on, you're going to stay a step or two ahead of anyone who wants to steal from you, mess with your life, or silence you online. All you have to do is what you're already doing—you're just going to do it a little smarter.

"Never sit at a table you can't walk away from."
—JOSS WHEDON

2. but it's just my phone number

You'd be surprised by how far one creep or criminal can get with your phone number. It's hard to believe that one little thing can cause so much trouble, but keeping your private life under wraps comes down to controlling certain pieces of information as much as you possibly can. You're about to find out exactly what information I'm talking about and how to protect all of it.

YOU CONTROL WHAT YOU SHARE

It's really important to safeguard pieces of personally identifying information, like your phone number, online. Social media and advertising companies are continually compiling dossiers on you, trying to match information across services

and devices in order to piece together the most complete profile they can. The more complete the info, the more valuable
it is when they sell it to and trade it with third parties. From
these third parties, your private information becomes public
in people-search databases. As if this weren't bad enough,
malicious hackers look for clues to your private information
in everything you do online.

The armor you build around that identifying information
protects every aspect of your privacy. Of course, what you do
in private or choose to share with friends is your own business.
But if you want to be confident that your information remains
personal, only share identifying info with people you trust.

For example, if you enjoy sex or explore aspects of your
sexual identity using technology, that experience should belong
to you. Only you should get to decide whether it was a good or
bad thing to do. Sexuality is one of the most important ways
in which we identify, establish, and maintain our boundaries.
Just as importantly, you should get to decide if that experience
(whether it's sharing intimate photos, talking dirty on the
phone or via voice chat, sexting, having any kind of online sex,
or just disclosing something on a sexual topic) gets shared with
anyone else. Personal information and experiences should be
private and under your control, unless you decide otherwise.
If you do decide to share that information, you should know
exactly what you're agreeing to.

PRIVATE SPACES AND ACTIVITIES

Private exploration, sexual and otherwise, is something we do
to better understand ourselves. We experiment with different
ideas about who we are and different ways of expressing our
identities. Sometimes, we may even play around with being
something (or someone) that we're not like at all in the real
world. Private spaces are where we get to safely figure out
who we are.

Privacy is critical to being able to decide what you like, discover what feels right and wrong for yourself, and find and keep your boundaries. That's just the truth and always has been. What's changed is the role technology plays in our private experiences. If you have a sexual moment in your room, that moment is still all yours unless you choose to share it. But when you have a private moment or experience online, you're taking a risk with your privacy.

Until the online revolution, our private spaces for exploration were our bedrooms and bathrooms, our homes, our phone calls, and our inner fantasy worlds. Now, those spaces can include texts, emails, photos, videos, and direct messages to trusted friends or family members. Online, private spaces include email inboxes, chat rooms, Internet Relay Chat (IRC), social media profiles, non-public messaging systems (Twitter direct messages [DMs], Facebook chat), dating websites, message boards, and all the places where your personal information resides. But those spaces are only private if you can really trust the people you share that information with.

For example, if you send or communicate something private while at work, at school, or even on Facebook, it might not be private because it might not actually be "yours" anymore— legally and, to some degree, practically speaking. The places where you experience private time online and on your phone are usually watched and monitored by the companies who host those services, too.

The problem is that not everyone understands or agrees on what constitutes a private space online, and some people don't know what information they need to protect and keep private. Even one piece of private information can unlock a trail that will expose most, if not all, of the other information it's attached to (just read Mat Honan's story in Chapter 3).

No one has a clear idea about which systems can be trusted completely, which systems should never be trusted, and which

systems to watch very carefully. Worse, many online companies, including some of the big ones you'd think you could
trust, have made it their business to take advantage of that
confusion and misplaced trust by leveraging privacy laws
that are way behind the times to collect, sell, and trade your
private information as data, in their databases. That's a
problem because it takes away your control over things that
could expose or hurt you, like your identifying information
and metadata (detailed background information on you) that
these companies collect when you use their services. The sad
fact is that these companies care about their bottom lines and
their corporate advertisers more than they do about you as a
consumer, so don't believe otherwise for a minute. Companies
like Twitter, Google, and Facebook need to convince you to
share your private information because their advertisers "need"
access to what rightfully belongs to you.

But you have a choice, and it's not your job to keep corpo-
rations wealthy by empowering them to invade your personal
space. Your private information and activities should remain
private, including all of the following:

- What you say or express in private chat or direct messages
- What you say or express in emails
- What you say or express on the phone
- What you say or express in your personal relationships
- Your text messages
- Personal photos that you share
- Your activity on dating websites
- Information related to your sexual activities and sexual
  orientation

- Information related to your health and medical records, including searches, doctor visits, and associated communications

- Information related to your gender identity

- Time you spend doing things that you want to keep to yourself

- Anything you keep in private files on your computer or phone

Next, I'll explain what information you should watch most closely and how to ensure that your private activities stay private.

LOCK DOWN YOUR PERSONALLY IDENTIFYING INFORMATION

Lots of things tempt us to give up our email address, phone number, physical address, ZIP code, and so on—sometimes harmlessly.

The information you should guard most closely is your *personally identifying information (PII)*, or just *personal information*. Even a few pieces of PII can be used to identify, contact, or locate you, allowing malicious people to attack you, stalkers to find you, and entities to get more information about you than you want to share. Companies like Facebook and Google use your PII for profit. Don't just give it away.

The following sections list what you should consider personal information, and each is named after a stoplight color so you can see which items are critical. The items on the red alert list can be used directly against you, and you should never give out or share these with any person, company, app, or website that you don't know or trust. The yellow alert list contains items that you should be very careful with because malicious hackers and stalkers can use them, but they can't hurt you with this information unless they have other pieces of information, too.

If anyone or any company asks for any of the items on your red or yellow lists, be on guard. But don't freak out if you've already given these things to other companies, no matter how shady they are. Even when things go screwy, it's almost never too late.

Red Alert List

Everything in this section can be used to directly hurt or harm you, steal your identity, make you physically unsafe, threaten or expose your loved ones, steal your money, or access your online accounts. *DON'T give this information out, and DON'T publish it online. DO keep close track of where it has been seen and who knows about it.*

Red alert items can't be changed (or are very hard to change) if something goes wrong, so you should watch what happens with everything on this list like a mama hawk:

- Passwords
- Real, full (family) name
- Address of your home, workplace, or school
- Social Security number
- Government ID numbers (driver's license number and passport number)
- Date and place of birth
- Biometric information (fingerprints, facial recognition, voice recognition)
- Computer's IP address (a unique number that identifies your computer on the Internet)

- Specific location (geolocation numbers, like those from your phone or in tagged photos)

- Credit and debit card numbers, security codes, and expiration dates

- Bank account numbers

- Answers to common security questions

Let's talk for a moment about those answers to common security questions. These can include your pet's name, your mother's maiden name, the city you were born in, and often other things that are easy to guess or dig up on your Facebook profile. A million years ago, when Paris Hilton's phone was hacked, the intruder reset her phone's password by getting one security question correct: her dog's name, which was findable on every gossip site in the world.

NOTE   *Credit card and bank account numbers are on the red list because while they can be changed, you can usually change them only after there has been a problem. Passwords can also be changed, but anyone who has them also has access to much of your red list information.*

Yellow Alert List

Yellow items can be used with other information to harm you, so avoid giving them out unless you trust the people or companies you share them with. If you choose to share them, keep a close eye on where they appear and who can see them.

Some yellow items can be changed if your personal information falls into evil hands, but changing them isn't easy:

- Name you use day to day, if different from your legal name

- Primary screen name(s)

- Email address (if it's not public)

- Telephone number

- Race, sexual orientation, and gender

- Mailing address (if it's different from your residence; otherwise it's red)

- Country, state, and city of residence

- ZIP code (or postal code)

- Google Voice number

Fortunately, you can make dummy versions of yellow items to use when you don't trust an app, website, social network, or person. Google Voice is on this list because if it's linked to your cell phone number, getting locked out of your Google account means that you'll be locked out of both numbers.

NOTE   *Even if yellow items are revealed to bad entities, they still won't sink your ship. Read more about making a dupe copy of your yellow items (and even some red items) in Chapter 9, "Ninja Tricks."*

If the red and yellow items seem like a lot to manage, or some of the items have already ended up "out there," don't worry. I'll show you how to fix and recover from those big and small privacy mistakes and how to manage your privacy easily going forward.

Green List

Items on your green list are okay to share. This list includes information about you that can't be used to hurt you or that's a dummy version of the real thing. For instance, if the numbers of your single-use credit card are stolen, you'll only lose the amount on the card. That's way better than losing a real credit card, which is tied to your credit score and often various online accounts and could cause a big headache.

Here are some examples of green items:

- Secondary screen names or account names (say, a throw-away email address that forwards to your primary address)

- Mailing address or PO box

- Digital, online phone number, such as a Skype number

- Email addresses that are not linked to a vital service, such as your bank account

- Photos and videos that don't embarrass you or reveal private information

- Social media profiles on sites where you're confident you understand the privacy settings

- General likes, favorites, and things you enjoy sharing on social media sites

- Single-use or gift credit cards

Apply the red, yellow, and green system to apps and online accounts to judge them for safety. An online account or app that asks for red information gets a red grade. If an app asks for a lot of red or yellow information but doesn't actually require that information in order to function, same thing: the site, account, or app is high risk. Even if it has the best security team in the world, it still gets the red or yellow rating because if it gets attacked, you're in more trouble (and have to do more post-attack cleanup in your life) than with a green app or account.

Information-Sharing Guidelines

As a rule, don't give out personally identifying information too readily. If you wouldn't give some bus driver or a creepy mall cop your home address and phone number, remember that just because websites ask for (or demand) personal info doesn't mean you have to give it to them. And you can often give fake information to get to the next screen.

Of course, you have to give real billing information when you buy things, but if you're registering with a free site that feels like it's getting too nosy about your business, give it fake information. You're not breaking any law under the sun if you do that. Just don't use someone else's real address; you'll definitely get in trouble for that.

Don't be fooled by websites that offer some sort of reward or prize in exchange for your contact information or other personal details. Usually, your name, browser and computer information, and email address are worth much more to them than whatever they're offering you because they can sell your information to other marketers, who will also resell it. You won't win an iPad, but the marketer will win a few more bucks if you give them your information. And female data sets are always worth more on the market than male ones, because women usually make more buying decisions and spend more money than men. (We're also worth more on the black market for seedy things like hacked webcam access, as mentioned in the story about Miss Teen USA in Chapter 1.)

A couple more things: avoid sending highly personal email to mailing lists and keep sensitive files only on your home computer. Your workplace or school is legally monitoring your Internet use and email on its network, so don't do anything private or sensitive in nature (like banking) on a work or school network. In most countries, employees have little if any privacy protection from monitoring by employers.

HE SAID, SHE SAID

Maybe you're thinking, "Eh, if my phone number gets in the wrong hands, it's really not that that big of a deal. I can always block the caller or hang up. Who cares, right?"

Let me tell you a story.

Every year in Germany, the world's longest-running hacker conference happens just after Christmas—Chaos Communication Congress (CCC). My bosses at CBS have never seen a great reason for me to fly from San Francisco to Hamburg to find news at some hacker gathering to report on over the holidays, when they're all away from the office with their families on the US East Coast. But one year, my interest in hackers and cybercrime got my editors to pay attention to my trip.

I was on my way to the airport Christmas Eve when I got some cryptic Twitter messages from hackers who had told the popular photo-sharing service Snapchat (which supposedly "disappears" your photos after you send them) that the service had a security problem. Snapchat ignored the hackers' warning.

Those same hackers messaged me to say they had found more serious problems with Snapchat and they had written a blog post about it. Right after I broke the news for CBS, malicious hackers took the user information—which included the name they registered with, username (handle), and phone number—and published all of it online.

On the long flight to CCC, I started chatting with a woman seated next to me about the news story. I explained that parts of Snapchat's huge user information database had been posted online for anyone to download and rifle through, and that the guys who ran Snapchat didn't seem to care.

She asked me whether names, phone numbers, email addresses, or even passwords were online. I told her that as far as we could tell, it was only usernames and phone numbers so far.

Her boyfriend, seated on the other side of the aisle, was listening, and he chose that moment to chime in. "Phone numbers and names? That's it?" he said. "Oh if it's just phone numbers and our names, whatever."

His girlfriend didn't agree. It was awkward.

This could have been a story about any app, or any of a zillion privacy breaches in the past couple of years. It isn't a story about "right" or "wrong" ways of thinking about privacy. Their reactions just show a great example of the difference between what women and men see as risky exposure. He didn't think it was a big deal for anyone to have his number, username, and real name. She, on the other hand, said it made her worried.

What my seatmate's boyfriend didn't consider is that he could also be a stalking victim—straight guys attract psychos, too. Creeps and stalkers come in all genders and sexual orientations. Men tend to feel a greater sense of physical and social safety, but that feeling is often illusory. Men are victims of malicious activity online all the time, as I'll describe in Chapter 3 with journalist Mat Honan's story.

WORST-CASE SCENARIO

The sad fact is that women have more reasons to be concerned about online privacy than men do, because women are at greater risk for physical violence and are directly targeted more often than men.

What's the worst thing that usually happens to a man's phone number? Someone posts it on Craigslist (or 4chan) in a "call and talk dirty to me" ad. A malicious hacker could then use it to try to reset a password or to try to steal the person's identity (which is actually pretty bad).

But think about what could happen to a woman. Identity theft is awful, but it's not the worst thing. Say you have an online enemy, like an ex or any psycho who's angry, missing you a little too much, unhinged, drunk and upset, or bent on revenge. If that person knows or even suspects that you use a particular online app like Facebook or Twitter, they can search the app using the information they have (any piece of a real name, username, or phone number) to see if they can find your current information.

Once they get more real information about your world, that stalker, creep, or vengeful ex gets closer to you. They can use your information to try to see what you're up to or, worse, to spy on you, stalk you, or harass you—whether as their real self or with a fake account. Once a heartbroken ex or stalker knows what account to zero in on, they may create a fake account and "friend" you.

Now they can track, harass, bully, and scare you. They can search for your username on other social media sites and apps, like photo sites where you post pictures of your boyfriend, family, pets, school, travels, and workplace. They can search social media sites for a history of your relationships, meaningful or painful experiences, and more. They can use location-tracking websites to follow you and your friends and family. The ways in which companies have woven together our identifying information online means that something as basic as your phone number needs to be protected more than ever.

When that stalker gets your phone number, you're in trouble. With that number in hand, that bad person can call you, find you in online databases, make changes to your accounts and services, or even hack your voicemail.

And it doesn't end there: anyone bent on vengeance will add your number to the dossier they're building about you, likely with the intent to publish it online later, along with your name, usernames, email addresses, and a list of online apps, accounts, and businesses you use. And I'm not talking about signing you up for magazine subscriptions and pizza deliveries, though jerks will do that, too.

I don't have to tell you that exes and stalkers do bad things in real life when they get close enough to the person they're obsessed with. If the malicious creep has posted things online about you to ruin your reputation, like impersonating you or publishing revenge porn of any kind, they could add your phone number to this awful public smear campaign—putting you at serious risk for more stalking and attacks from others.

"I don't do damsel in distress very well. It's hard for me to play a victim."—SCARLETT JOHANSSON

3. you got hacked

Contrary to sensationalist news stories, malicious hackers don't always launch attacks to make a political statement or to get attention: most do it for the money. They want your phone number or other personal information because they can use it to steal your identity (among other ways of monetizing the data) and anything in an account that uses your phone number as a login or for security questions. In this chapter, I'll explain why someone might steal your personal information, how to prevent that from happening, and what to do if it does happen to you.

Names, usernames, and other personally identifying information are worth money on the black market. They get sold to data brokers, who add the info to bigger databases to be matched with more of your information. That pool of information is then resold to people who sell it yet again as people-finder services—and to people who make money off of identity theft.

How can malicious hackers use a single phone number to totally own your life? It might seem like dark magic involving voodoo candles and computer masterminds, but all an attacker really needs to do is figure out how to play different websites' password resets off each other in a kind of daisy chain.

It's almost child's play. In fact, it took one attacker only one hour to destroy the digital life of *Wired* journalist Mat Honan. Before Honan could grasp what was going on, his attacker remotely erased (forever) everything on his iPhone, iPad, and MacBook, including photos of deceased in-laws and the first year of his daughter's life. That attacker also deleted Honan's Google account and took over his Twitter account to post a bunch of racist and homophobic tweets under his name.

Honan realized something was wrong when he was playing with his daughter and suddenly his iPhone restarted and asked for a four-digit PIN. He knew he hadn't set the phone up with a PIN.

ONE COMPROMISED ACCOUNT TO RULE THEM ALL

Making an amazing bunch of passwords wouldn't have saved Honan, because his attacker didn't run a program to crack or brute-force his password. They weren't using some crazy-advanced, hacker-voodoo program. The attacker simply reset the password on just one of Honan's online accounts, thanks to a seemingly harmless piece of personally identifying information: a street address. Then the attacker went to town resetting and taking over the rest of Honan's accounts.

Honan's Amazon account went first, when his attacker fooled Amazon's tech support into revealing part of a credit card number in his billing information. The attack was easy enough: the attacker just called Amazon, gave Honan's name and billing address, and added a new credit card to the account. Then, the attacker called Amazon again, said they'd lost access to "their" account (actually Mat's account), and provided the new credit card number as proof of identity. Amazon let the attacker add a new email address to Honan's account, and from there they just logged in, changed the main password, and started using the information saved in Amazon account to set to work on Honan's Apple account.

When this particular attack occurred, Amazon showed customers the same four digits of their credit card numbers that Apple used to verify identities and release account information. The four digits that Amazon didn't hide were the same ones that Apple hid, so the attacker had enough information from Amazon to get into Honan's Apple ID account. Once in, they wiped his devices. Next, they used the information they had acquired to do a Gmail password reset, which gave them access to Honan's Twitter account—their true goal. Game over.

WHAT HONAN DID WRONG

All Honan's attacker needed to crack his Apple account was an email address, the last four digits of a credit card on file, and the card's billing address. Honan's Gmail and Apple accounts were linked, allowing the attacker to see the credit card digits from Honan's Amazon account. The final piece, Honan's billing address, was publicly available: a whois lookup* on Honan's website (which lacked privacy controls that would have hidden his address) did the job.

---

* A *whois lookup* (pronounced "who is") is the name for a query and response protocol—a tool—used to look up the ownership information on a website. To use a whois lookup, you enter a web address into the tool's search form, and the tool gives you all the public information associated with that website, such as the owner's name, address, and phone number. Most domain registration companies (such as GoDaddy, Dotster, or HostGator) let you make your information private for a fee, which keeps it out of easy public reach. If you haven't activated account privacy on websites you've registered, do it now—and make sure everyone who shares an address with you has done it for all of their sites as well.

Both Amazon and Apple have since closed the holes that allowed the devastating attack on Honan, but bad security practices are everywhere online. Honan lost his photos forever because he didn't store backup copies elsewhere for safekeeping. He inadvertently gave his attackers access by linking his Gmail and Apple accounts. All his email addresses used the same user ID (*mhonan*), and the email address he used for account and password recovery was part of his Google account. His iPhone and computer were remotely wiped because he had set up Find My Mac, which a lot of people use.

Honan's story sounds like a complicated mess, and it was, but you can learn from his mistakes.

HACK-PROOF YOUR LIFE

The good news is that Honan's mistakes are avoidable. Here are some easy things you can do to try to prevent attacks on your personal information and accounts.

Make Your Address Hard to Find

If you have a website, make sure you have whois privacy turned on. If the company your domain or website is registered with doesn't offer this feature, change registrars right away and hide that information. Next, remove your address from people-search websites. (Chapter 7 and the Resources section will help you do this.)

Don't Link Major Accounts

Some apps want you to link your Facebook, Twitter, Flickr, Instagram, and other accounts with them. The problem is, if all of those accounts are linked, someone needs to crack only that one app to have access to all of those accounts. If you do choose to link your accounts, make sure each is an information dead end for malicious attackers. And think twice before allowing online apps access to accounts like those hosted by Google and Apple, which probably contain a lot of sensitive information.

Don't Use One Service for Everything

As tempting as it is to use one company and one email account for everything online (or as much as Google might try to make you), you're much safer if you use different services for your important stuff. For instance, if you have Google Voice linked to your phone number, use Google Calendar and Google docs for work and personal stuff, have Gmail as your main email, and store all of your contacts and addresses with Google, then you're screwed if your Gmail account is compromised. If you get hacked and lose your Google account, you'll find it hard to get it back, and it can take days to do so. First you'll feel violated and robbed, but then you'll feel like Google is holding you hostage.

If this happens to you, keep reading: resources and information about the account-recovery process are provided later in this chapter and will help you start the process of getting your life back. But this is why it's so important to prepare in case you get hacked. Protect yourself—diversify your stuff.

Back Up Your Everything:
Your Contacts, Your Files, Your Photos

Back up everything. Use a secure backup hard drive that you keep at home (or in another safe place), or keep your backups on a computer that's separate from all others. CrashPlan is an example of a backup service that copies and stores your files on a regular schedule, and it also comes as stand-alone software. Don't use a friend or family member's computer for backups because not only do you risk them looking at your stuff, but if they're compromised, your stuff is at risk, too.

You might consider backing up your files to a cloud service like Dropbox, Box, or Amazon, but if you do, make sure to separate that account from all other accounts by giving it a different username and password.

Encrypt Your Computer's Hard Drive

Encryption lets you protect your electronic information with a virtually uncrackable password, and Windows, Mac, iOS, and Android all offer ways to encrypt your local storage. Search online to find out how to turn encryption on for your system. Look for Apple's built-in encryption program FileVault and BitLocker on Windows. Without encryption, anyone with a few minutes of access to your computer, tablet, or smartphone can spy on, copy, or steal your files, even if they don't have your password.

Ultimately, you should watch your personal information like a hawk and keep an eye out for unusual activity. Something is probably wrong if your accounts start sending password resets you know you didn't initiate or if you start getting account-recovery emails. And beware of account-recovery emails for accounts you know are not yours: these are probably fake phishing emails designed to trick you into clicking links and entering passwords, inadvertently revealing your information or allowing the installation of malware on your computer.

If things go wrong in spite of taking these precautions, you can still minimize the damage. I'll tell you how in the next section.

WHAT TO DO WHEN YOU'VE BEEN ATTACKED

There are two main ways you can be the victim of malicious hacking: you can be personally targeted, or you can be the victim of a company that follows bad security practices.

NOTE   *To see if your information was released in a recent breach of a company's website, visit* http://www.haveibeenpwned.com/.

If you think your accounts have been attacked, try to access those accounts. If you're able to log in, reset the passwords if possible, and check all settings carefully in case an attacker added a forwarding address for all of your email or changed your security questions. Check everything.

In particular, if your email account is attacked, follow these steps:

1. Change your password.
2. Change your username if possible.
3. Look through your inbox for unusual activity.
4. Check sent email for suspicious activity, and see what you find in the Trash.
5. See if any users or email addresses have been added to the account and delete any you don't recognize.
6. Look for email forwarding. If you didn't turn it on, turn it off.
7. Check every single setting. If you're not sure what a particular setting means, search for it online. Also look for settings that just look wrong or out of place.
8. If any of your contacts have been sent emails that were not from you, contact them immediately. Warn them that your account has been compromised and not to respond to or click anything in those emails. Let them know too that you have the situation under control.

Follow any relevant steps in the list above for all of the accounts you can access. You may still be locked out of some accounts at this point, but don't panic. You can get them back.

Recover Your Accounts and Data

Next, contact websites for which you're unable to reset passwords, and follow their account-recovery processes. Many, like Twitter and Google, will have online forms you can fill out or other procedures to follow when you've been locked out of your account.

For example, Google will ask you questions that only you can answer, like which five people you email most often. After a day or so, you should receive an email that sends you to a page where you have to answer more questions about your Google account, such as the names of your folders, when you started using different Google services, and so on. Getting your Google account back can take at least 48 hours, often longer.

Google may not be known for customer service, and neither is Yahoo!, Hotmail, or any other "free" online business. But you'll have to put up with them to get your accounts back, and here's a short list of forms and phone numbers to get you started. (For help finding direct phone numbers that may save you a ton of time, check out *http://gethuman.com/*.)

- **Amazon:** Use **Help ▸ Contact Us**.

- **Apple:** Reset your Apple ID password at *http://iforgot .apple.com/password/verify/appleid/*, or find your Apple ID at *http://iforgot.apple.com/appleid/*.

- **eBay:** Call 1.866.961.9253. Tell them you'd like to talk about "Account—someone has used your account."

- **Facebook:** *http://facebook.com/hacked/*

- **Google:** *http://google.com/accounts/recovery/*

- **Microsoft** (Outlook, Xbox, Hotmail, and so on): *http:// account.live.com/acsr/*

- **PayPal:** 1.888.221.1161 (Outside the United States, call 1.402.935.2050.)

- **Twitter:** *http://support.twitter.com/forms/hacked/*

- **Yahoo!:** *http://help.yahoo.com/kb/helpcentral/* or
  1.800.318.0612

You'll have to look hard to find support for some websites, and others may have nothing to help you. If you don't see what you need in the list here, search online for "[website] account verification form" or "[website] account hacked," or go to the website's help or contact page.

When you contact a company, be prepared with your account details or other personal information. Don't expect all companies to be uniformly helpful, no matter how big they are or how many fans they have. When Honan tried to contact Apple for help, Apple support was useless, even though he had AppleCare. He ultimately took his Mac in to an Apple Store while it was still being remotely wiped (the wipe takes a while), and an employee was able to stop the wipe from progressing.

Once you recover your accounts, follow the same steps as in "What to Do When You've Been Attacked" on page 36 for accounts you didn't have to recover. Yes, it's a pain, and it'll take a while, but it's worth your time and effort. For example, Honan had to borrow a friend's computer so he could reset his Apple password. From there, he used iCloud backups to restore his phone and laptop. It took seven hours to restore his phone, but eventually he got his life back.

Attackers will often delete your data after they've gone through it, too. Don't be surprised if you go into your compromised accounts and find that all of your emails, contacts, photos, and other data have been erased. By the way, if you ever have a hard drive wiped as a result of an attack, take your computer to a place that specializes in hard drive recovery to try to recover some of your data. Only go to reputable places, like DriveSavers, and expect a price tag around $1,500 or more.

Once you have your accounts back and secured, you may be able to restore your contacts and any other data from backups. If you don't have backups, let people know what you've lost (like their contact information or files you've shared), so they can help you start getting your life back on track.

Even if you never get attacked personally, a company you trust with sensitive data could be breached, leaving your information exposed. In that case, follow the steps I describe next.

When a Service Gets Hacked

In February 2014, I reported for ZDNet.com that Comcast had been breached and the company had ignored the attack. I warned that Comcast customers were at risk of losing their email accounts to identity theft, with potential financial repercussions. Unfortunately, Comcast never told its users that their sensitive account information might have been leaked.

A lot of Comcast users asked me what they should do. I gave a checklist of minimum requirements to be safe and suggestions for users who want to be very, very careful. This is a good checklist of what to change after a service you use has been compromised.

At the very least, you should change passwords for the following:

- All services and email accounts belonging to the breached business, especially ones tied to your main account

- Services or accounts that use the hacked account's email address as the username. For instance, if Comcast is attacked and you use your *<name>@comcast.net* email address anywhere, change the passwords to those sites.

To be extra careful, change these, too:

- The master account's username (eHow has tutorials for services such as Comcast.)

- Passwords to any connected billing systems and to services with the same password as the one you used for the compromised service

- The username of any account that uses the compromised email address as its username

I also suggested that victims of a breach log in to any billing accounts connected to the breached service (like an autopay bank account or a credit card) and, if possible, add an alert for unusual activity. If a data breach affects you, it's a good idea to personally monitor your connected billing accounts frequently for unusual activity. Even if you're not a victim, make sure your autopay account has some kind of safeguard against fraudulent activity, just in case.

And if you're ever the victim of a company's data breach, fill out the claim form on the Federal Trade Commission (FTC) website so you have something official in hand should your accounts be used for criminal activity. (Visit *http://ftc complaintassistant.gov/* and click **Identity Theft**.) If enough claim forms are submitted, the compromised company may be held accountable through class-action lawsuits, which you may want to join. Many companies have also begun to offer free credit monitoring to affected customers.

When a service that you trusted with your financial information experiences a data breach, watch your financial accounts closely. If you notice suspicious behavior, take action immediately. Learn more about this in the next section.

IF YOUR FINANCIAL INFORMATION MAY HAVE BEEN EXPOSED IN A DATA BREACH

If you suspect that your bank information, credit cards, PayPal account, or any other financial apps or services may have been compromised by a data breach, contact your bank and credit card companies about your accounts right away. Change your passwords for any at-risk accounts and ask the companies to monitor your accounts for fraud.

If a company won't put a watch on your account (I've had customer service people at credit card companies say they don't), be sure to write down the time, date, and person you talked to when you tried to alert the company about suspicious activity. Then, monitor your accounts for unauthorized transactions. The FTC recommends that you close any credit card accounts that you know have been compromised.

If you close a checking account, keep in mind that checks you've written may be returned, and recent transactions may bounce. If you use an automatic bill payment system or have set up debits from your bank account, update your account profile information to reflect your changes. Do the same for your PayPal account or similar online payment and banking accounts.

If you're a US citizen and the information exposed includes your Social Security number, use the following information to contact the three major credit bureau companies and place a fraud alert on your report:

- **Equifax:** 1.800.525.6285; *http://equifax.com/*; PO Box 740241, Atlanta, GA 30374-0241

- **Experian:** 1.888.397.3742; *http://experian.com/*; PO Box 2002, Allen, TX 75013

- **TransUnion:** 1.800.680.7289; *http://transunion.com/*; Fraud Victim Assistance Division, PO Box 6790, Fullerton, CA 92834-6790

With a fraud alert in place, banks and credit bureaus will know they should contact you to verify applications for new accounts because of a higher likelihood for fraud.

If information from your driver's license, state ID, passport, employer or student ID, Social Security card, or any other government ID is stolen, replace the ID right away and tell the agency that issued it what happened. That way, the agency can prevent someone else from using your name to get a fake ID.

Now that you know which accounts you should definitely change if you get hacked, let's revisit one that you don't have to change but might want to anyway: your email address.

HOW TO CHANGE YOUR EMAIL ADDRESS

Once you've reset your password and taken all the steps I outline under "What to Do When You've Been Attacked" on page 36, you don't need to dump your email provider, but you may want to if you think there are security issues or if it will make you feel better. Maybe your email provider handled the security breach badly. If they ignored the problem or only told you about it after you heard about it elsewhere, it's time to move.

NOTE   *Many people say that it's better and safer to have your own domain and host your own email. That's fine if you know how, but most people don't—and that's okay. Having your email at, say, Gmail, where it's Google's job to keep you secure, is a million times better than trying to learn to manage it yourself.*

To change your email address, take the following steps:

1. Pick a new email provider, and set up a new account.
2. Set up email forwarding at the old email address.
3. Set up an "I've moved" autoresponse at the old email address.
4. Import your old email, and transfer your address book, calendars, any linked documents, and so on.
5. Make a list of accounts to update, including banks, payment accounts, social media, mailing lists, and so on.
6. Email all your contacts with your new email address.
7. Shut down your old email after six months.

I'll walk you through each step in this section, so let's jump right in.

Choose a New Home

Which new email provider you choose will depend on what features you'd like the new service to have, whom you'll trust more than the old guys, and what you want in the new address itself. For instance, a Google address will have *@gmail.com* after the name you pick, but Gmail will also let you make emails appear to come from a completely different email address, one that you specify (from a different account that you import or from an alias that you set up in Gmail).

Here are a few email providers to consider:

- Gmail

- Microsoft Outlook

- Yahoo! Mail

- iCloud

- Hushmail

- Zoho Mail

Whatever your needs, make sure you can access your new email service from anywhere, including any computer, your phone, and so on. Don't be tempted to use an address you were given by a school, a workplace, an organization, or an Internet service provider (ISP). These services aren't a long-term solution, and you definitely won't be as safe from malicious hackers as you would be if you used email hosted by Microsoft Outlook or Gmail.

NOTE   *When setting up an email address, remember that bigger companies generally care more about their email security reputation than do smaller organizations and often have more battle-tested and up-to-date security.*

When selecting an email provider, choose a major company that offers web-based email, and make sure it uses *Secure Sockets Layer (SSL)* to send email securely. SSL establishes an encrypted link between a web server and a browser, creating a secure connection. You can tell when a website uses SSL because the address bar (where the URL appears) will show *https* instead of *http*. If a service doesn't use SSL, it's not taking your security seriously at all.

That said, there are downsides to using free, browser-based email services. The main problem is that certain changes, like redesigns, can screw up your entire inbox or worse. For example, what if Google decides to rearrange your address book because it thinks it knows what you need better than you do? If you pay for an email service and have your own domain name, you can switch providers and still own your stuff if something goes wrong.

And now a word about email addresses: pick one that will stand the test of time! If you pick one with a date in it, or something silly, people may not take you seriously when you send email about something serious. (For example, if you send an email asking to have revenge porn removed from an address that tells the sender you're *sexkitten2009*, you might not get the response you were looking for.)

Once you settle on a service and choose an address, it's time to start using your new email.

Set Up Forwarding

When changing email providers, find out if your current email provider will allow your old address to forward mail to the new one. That way, you won't have to keep logging in to your old account to check your mail. If your old provider doesn't forward, don't panic: just set a reminder to check your old email address every day for a week, then twice a week for a month, and then twice a month until your six-month transition is over.

Whether you forward your email or not, set up an autoresponder (also called a vacation responder or autoreply) at your old address. Just write a short message telling senders that your email has changed and what the new address is. Every time anyone emails you, they'll get a reminder to update your email address. But be sure to email your contacts directly, too, to let them know that your email address has changed.

Move In

Next, transfer your address book to your new account, or you'll have to start collecting friends' email addresses all over again. You'll usually find that you can easily migrate your old contacts and emails to your new email address. Look for tutorials online that are specific to your old email service and the one you're moving to. Email services try to make it easy for you to move in and difficult for you to leave, so the one who wants your business usually has workarounds for the guy who won't let you go. If your new service sets up email forwarding automatically, you don't even need to worry about setting up forwarding at the old account.

No matter what, definitely copy (back up) all your emails and your address book from your old account, just in case something goes wonky when you move them. Each email provider has slightly different back-up or download steps, so search online for the ones specific to your situation.

Some email transitions are really easy: for example, Outlook lets you migrate everything over from Gmail with just a few clicks. Go to **Settings** and look at **Accounts** in both services. Go into your old email account, and look for the setting to establish forwarding and create autoresponses (such as vacation responses) to start sending mail to your new address. In your new email account, find where it lets you check mail from or add other accounts to start having your old account's email routed to your new address.

Adding an account should import all of your old email into your new account, and you'll start to get any new emails that come through. Once you're happy with all your new email account settings, turn your attention to your other online accounts.

Update Your Accounts

Log in to each of your online accounts, from Facebook to your bank, and update your email address. This process will probably be the biggest chore of all, so be systematic: make a list and go through the accounts, one by one.

To help create your list, search your old email account for terms like *subscribe, account,* and *login.* If you use a password manager like 1Password, you actually have a list of sites already, tied to your passwords. (And don't forget to update the information about your new email address in your password manager!)

Tell Everyone

Now use your new address to send an email to everyone in your address book, including friends, relatives, and business and school associates, telling them your new address. Say something like this:

> *Hi there. This is my new email address, and I'll be using it from now on. Please update your address book. Thank you!*

Send the message to yourself (again, with the new address) and bcc everyone else on your list. The bcc part is extremely important. If you don't put everyone in the bcc field, all recipients (that's everyone in your address book!) will see everyone else's email addresses, and if anyone hits "reply to all," they'll email the other recipients, too. Most people think this is a huge invasion of privacy, and it will make almost everyone really mad at you.

Now enjoy your new email address. Hopefully it's a with better service than the one you left. Leaving an old, outdated, or problematic service behind can help you feel safer and more in control, as well as give you the great feeling of moving on.

In the next chapter, I'll explore more about why it can feel good to start fresh with a new service.

"I learned early that I had to work harder than the white kids and harder than the boys." —Queen Latifah

4. female trouble

The term "driving while black" refers to the fact that African-American drivers in the United States are much more likely than white people to get pulled over or otherwise singled out by authorities simply on the basis of suspicion or just for harassment. The expression's been adapted to refer to similar forms of prejudice, like "flying while Muslim," and I think there needs to be a related term: "online while female." Women are more likely than men to be singled out online for stalking, harassment, invasions of privacy, and threats of physical violence.

When a woman gets hacked, she's got a lot more to lose, and if Mat Honan were a woman, you can be almost certain that his experience of getting severely hacked would have been different. Not only would a girl go through everything

Honan experienced, but on top of all that, she would also be subjected to gender targeting and all the ugly stuff that goes along with it.

Think about your intimate photos of yourself, ranging from swimsuit shots and selfies with cleavage to the photos and videos that are meant only for the eyes of a person you trust. Such photos, in the hands of someone who doesn't care about you or your safety (or worse, someone who gets off on hurting women), are disastrous, no matter how proud you are of your body, how sex-positive you may be, or how comfortable you feel with being sexy and strong at the same time.

In this chapter, I'll show you how to take charge of a situation in which your private content has been posted online maliciously or an attacker has otherwise attempted to compromise your reputation. This happens to people of all genders, but not as much as it happens to girls. Our gender makes us targets. Being "online while female" isn't fair, but it's a fact. Here's how you can fight back.

RECOVERING FROM HARASSMENT

When someone takes your personal photos and posts them online, it's not a joke. It's harassment and a (very) personal attack. Yet some people will try to make you feel like this kind of attack is somehow your fault. Don't ever—*ever*—listen to anyone who tells you that just because you're a girl, you're "asking for it" online (or offline). Some people will say that you shouldn't take nude selfies at all if you don't want them to be misused, as if taking a photo of yourself naked is some twisted way of asking to be punished for it. But we don't deserve to lose our jobs, our friends, custody of our kids, our personal safety, our emotional well-being, or our mental health for doing what hundreds of celebrities do on Twitter every week (or what a million creepy dudes do on Twitter every day with their own dick pics).

Telling a victim, "you shouldn't have done it" or "what did you expect?" is pointless, unfair, stupid, and just plain wrong. Instead of blaming and shaming, how about some information you can really use to help you make the decisions that are right for you? I'll equip you with tools to mitigate, minimize, and possibly even avoid damage if something goes wrong.

Do this when you're targeted:

- Stay calm online, don't blame yourself, and take steps to strengthen your mental and emotional health in real life. Eat, sleep, and seek support from friends who care about you or even from a skilled therapist. (Find a list of therapists who "get" tech issues at *http://smartprivacy .tumblr.com/therapists/*.)

- Keep your social media accounts open, instead of quitting the Internet. They'll be valuable tools later. It's okay to change your account settings to private if you prefer. Some sites (such as Twitter) have simple on/off-style privacy settings, and others (like Facebook) have more-nuanced options for limiting access to your profile. And don't be afraid to be heavy-handed with blocking profiles that bother you: block anyone, anytime, and you'll feel much better for doing so.

- File a police report to put the harassment on the record, but don't expect the police to do anything.

- Talk to a lawyer if you want to explore the possibility of pursuing legal action. Find a directory at *http:// withoutmyconsent.org/*.

- Find all the websites, social media accounts, and forums containing your private images and videos.

- Make detailed records of everything you find: take screencaps; for each image, note the date and time of posting and the screen name of the person that posted it; download all the photos you find (they have hidden data on them); and save everything in a folder.

- Get the images taken down (see "Getting Your Private Photos Offline" on page 59).

- Consider paying a reputation service to help reduce the harm.

Online harassment increases your vulnerability to sexual violence, can cause real emotional harm, and can ruin your reputation. This harassment sends the message that women are inferior, sexual objects. It communicates to the world that it's okay to devalue us and invites others to participate in harassing, humiliating, and hurting us.

There are so many real-life examples of all the types of harm I've described that going into detail would fill this book and so many more. (It would be the start of the most horrifying and depressing library in the world.) There are dozens of news stories about schoolteachers who've lost their jobs after their nude or swimsuit photos were posted online. Take, for example, the Christian schoolteacher who lost her job in 2013 after her nude selfies were stolen from her phone and linked with her name. In the same year, a female firefighter in Manchester (UK) lost her job for posing in lingerie for a shutterbug friend—even though her male firefighter coworkers had posed for racy firemen calendars.

The harm is real. In fact, the psychological and emotional damage of violating a girl's privacy like this can kill her. In 2013, a 17-year-old girl in Brazil committed suicide after a video of her being sexual with two friends was posted online; she was depressed and angry for the month leading up to her suicide. That same year, a California girl killed herself after a video of her being raped while passed out was sent around at her high school. And countless girls have been blackmailed and threatened into having sex or paying money to avoid the online publication of private images and videos. That's just what happened to Miss Teen USA in 2013 when her webcam was hacked.

But the negative emotions won't last forever, and there are ways to cope.

When Will It Stop?

Having your privacy violated in ways that are specific to being a girl is extremely painful. It feels so personal, so awful, and so unfair—because it is. Online privacy violations can cause all the same reactions an in-person violation would.

Here are things you might feel:

- Anxiety and fear

- Detachment, as if you're an outsider to your own life

- Intense distress

- Unsafe, even when it makes no sense to feel this way

- Irritability

- Anger

- Guilt, shame, and self-blame

- Mistrust and betrayal

- Depression and hopelessness

- Alienation and loneliness

- Embarrassment and exposure

    And here are some things you might experience:

- Intrusive, upsetting thoughts or memories that can come on suddenly

- Unreliable memory, such as difficulty remembering exact details

- Nightmares and insomnia

- Physical reactions such as a pounding heart, rapid breathing, nausea, muscle tension, or sweating

- Difficulty concentrating

- Avoidance of people, events, or situations

It's okay to feel and experience all these things—they're normal reactions. If you're a victim of any kind of violation, make sure you show this list to the people who care about you so they know what you're going through. Reading the list will give them an idea of what's going on if you get depressed, snap at them out of the blue, or toss and turn in bed. It'll also help people understand so they can give you the support and room you need to conquer this madness and, finally, heal.

These feelings are like storms; they come in and rage for a while, and they go back out to sea again. You may only feel some of the things mentioned here, or you may feel all of them. You may even feel confusing things sometimes, and many girls who've been violated (whether online or in real life) find they repeatedly cycle through these feelings.

These feelings are a lot like grief. Sometimes, just when you feel like you're doing okay, one trigger will bring back that feeling in your chest or your stomach, and the emotional spiral begins again. You might feel like it will never end, but it will. The annoying part is that there won't be one single moment when the way you feel inside just ends. But one day, you'll realize that you haven't felt upset in a long time, and that's when you'll know you're through it.

Until then, here are some ways to deal with those feelings.

Staying Strong

Without My Consent (*http://withoutmyconsent.org/*), a resource for legal options regarding stalking, revenge porn, and online harassment, describes steps you can take on the road to emotional recovery:

> *Taking active, practical steps to address the problem can help. Consulting with an attorney or law enforcement officers is important if someone has threatened you. It's also important to see what*

practical and legal steps you can take to combat the invasion of your privacy. Although a formal complaint process may increase your feelings of stress while it is ongoing, this kind of active coping with the situation helps some people feel better more quickly.

Addressing your feelings is important, too. Talking to people who care about you can help, as can talking to a counselor or therapist. Joining a support group may also comfort you and allow you to feel safer. Keeping a journal where you put your feelings into words also works for some people.

Doing things every day—especially small things—that make you feel good (for example, exercising, experiencing natural beauty, gardening) is important, as is finding a way to relax. Many people also find religious or spiritual practices help them cope with these kinds of painful experiences. Try not to rely on drugs, alcohol, or caffeine, as these substances can make things worse.

If the way you feel just won't let up, and if it gets in the way of your important relationships, jeopardizes your job or schoolwork, or keeps you from functioning normally (especially if you feel like you just can't take it any longer), reach out to someone who will help you weather your storms until they're gone. Find someone to talk to who has experience working with trauma, harassment, or abuse. If you want some psychological support, these resources are great:

- **Breakthrough.com:** Confidential online counseling, therapy, and assessments

- **American Psychological Association, Psychology Help Center:** *http://apa.org/helpcenter/*

- **eTherapi.com:** Reputable, secure website and network where you can talk to a therapist online

- **National Association of Social Workers:** Tips on finding a therapist and resource links; *http://helpstartshere .org/find-a-social-worker/*

- **American Counseling Association:** Counselor and therapist locators; *http://counseling.org/*

- **Rape, Abuse & Incest National Network:** Sexual assault and sexual trauma help resources; *http://rainn .org/get-help/* or 1.800.656.HOPE [4673]

- **Tech Savvy Therapists:** A growing resource of therapists who "get" issues surrounding technology and online problems; some will do online sessions; *http://smartprivacy .tumblr.com/therapists/*

What's most important is that you find someone you feel safe enough with to talk about what's happened and what you're going through. As soon as you feel ready, though, it's time to take back control of your personal content and online image from the ones who hurt you.

FIGHTING BACK

You should know a few facts about getting your private photos and videos removed from a website or taken out of the public eye. First, you can probably do it; second, there are most likely fewer of them out there than you think; and third, this whole awful experience will pass like a bad storm. Don't let the situation get to you, and don't give up. You're going to win, so focus on staying strong. Keep records on everything you find and keep making content online, but manage your expectations: while there are more resources out there than ever before, you'll find that some options are flat-out inadequate.

Navigating the Legal System

There are a few legal paths to justice, but no, you probably can't successfully sue a website where someone else has posted photos of you. Section 230 of the Communications Decency Act protects websites from legal liability arising from most content uploaded by their users. Some women have tried to sue websites, and they've almost all lost (except for one case in which a Yahoo! representative said the company would take something down and then broke that promise).

The laws around the publication of intimate and private photos online without the subject's consent are a mess. The rules themselves and the results you can obtain differ from country to country and from state to state in the United States, and even between civil and criminal federal laws. It's easy to feel overwhelmed, but there are websites to help you understand what you can and can't do, such as Without My Consent (*http://withoutmyconsent.org/*) and End Revenge Porn (*http://endrevengeporn.org/*). Make sure you talk to at least three lawyers before making a decision about how to move forward. Choose one who doesn't make you feel bad, ashamed, or like any of this is your fault.

If you're in the United States, ask your lawyer about the different angles you might consider pursuing, including intentional infliction of emotional distress, negligence, stalking, breach of contract, and invasion of privacy claims.

And keep this in mind: many women end up not being able to use the legal system. It's extremely expensive, it draws more attention to you, it's incredibly brutal for your emotional state, and it will reveal your identity even further. Often, the legal system can't even do that much to help you. (The deck is also stacked against you in court if your attacker is broke; you won't be able to get damages from someone who has no money.)

But you can accomplish some things through the legal system. In addition to awarding monetary damages, courts can provide injunctive relief (court orders) that can require your attacker to stop doing something. Depending on the laws you're dealing with, you might be able to get a court order that requires the attacker to stop posting images or videos or to take down images that have already been posted.

Getting a Restraining Order

If you think you might be in physical danger from the attacker posting your private images or information, get a restraining order. Even if you don't think it will work, you need one on record if you're seriously afraid for your safety.

You can get a civil restraining order on your own, though a lawyer will make the process easier. Even if the court doesn't grant your request, it will document that you're having serious problems with someone harassing you. If you need to build a bigger case later, that paper trail will be critical. Because court proceedings are public records, your filing will also put a dent in your attacker's reputation.

Here's my story. I was cyberstalked, threatened, abused, and harassed online by two creeps (a man and a woman who met each other while attacking me) for over a year. They did this on every website where I had a public social media account, on websites that mentioned me, on news websites that published my work, and anywhere friends posted photos with me. They even created blogs to harass me and post private information about me online. For better or for worse, they used people-finder websites to source their personal information about me, and most of it was incorrect.

Though they lived in different states, they conspired (unsuc-cessfully) to get my social media accounts taken away and to post as much personal information about me as possible in blog post comments and photo comments. They even edited fake information into the Wikipedia page about me. They emailed threats directly to me, and they bragged online about stalking me. One of the stalkers told an email list that I was no longer on the list thanks to their stalking and harassment and that someone should take away my car. Shortly afterward my car was vandalized—twice.

When I filed for a restraining order against both of them, they published the restraining order filing to the Wikipedia page about me—with my address on it. It was 2007: the judge who oversaw the case said he didn't understand how a restraining order could apply to the Internet, and he didn't grant the order against my abusers on this technical point. I was among the first women to seek a legal path to justice for online harassment (a major reason why I'm on the advisory board for Without My Consent.) At least the judge didn't deny the need for both restraining orders, so he didn't dismiss them, and he ordered the filings kept open so I could reapply later.

Thankfully, times have changed, and judges now understand the harm and damage that online abusers can do. But even though I had a judge who didn't get it, the restraining order filing entered my abusers' names on police records. It also provided me with police reports that documented their stalking, harassment, and abuse. Those police files came in handy when I needed to protect myself from them again later and when I requested removal of my personal, private information from people-finder websites.

In California, if the person threatening you is your current or former lover, you can ask for a domestic violence restraining order. This order may prohibit the online attacker from coming within a certain distance of you, your home, and your workplace. Depending on exactly what the order says, the police might be able to arrest the online attacker if they violate the order offline.

Even once you take action against your harasser, however, there's still work to be done: it's time to get your personal content out of the public eye and polish your reputation back to its original shine.

GETTING YOUR PRIVATE PHOTOS OFFLINE

Having something removed doesn't mean it's actually gone. Many sites and apps keep things on their servers, and as of this writing, there's nothing anyone can do about it. But you can still get photos and videos out of the public eye. They'll fade quickly from memory, especially from the memory of search engines.

Getting content off sites and out of search results is like playing a game of Whac-A-Mole. One thing pops up, you deal with it, and then another thing pops up, and you have to deal with that. The process is annoying and exhausting. But you'll notice that it comes in waves, and each wave is smaller until, eventually, the whole thing fades away.

Believe it or not, you can make it fade away faster by increasing your online presence—making yourself more visible. In fact, a primary step in dealing with revenge porn or any other kinds of unwanted online content about you is *not* to delete your social media accounts. Don't disappear from the Internet! Instead, make as much noise as possible to drown out the search results you want to eliminate.

If you remove your social media accounts, your blog or blog posts, or your normal online presence, you'll allow the bad content to gradually replace any good search results you had going in the first place. It's okay to change your account settings to private for a while or close comments on posts and photos to reduce the stress—but stand your ground. Showing the online world who you really are—with dignity—is part of how you'll fight fire with fire.

Doing It Yourself

It's going to feel horrible, but you'll probably need to go find the images or videos and get them taken down yourself. The police won't do it, and you can do the most damage control if you're the only one who knows what was put online, and where it is. You'll need to find all images and videos and send each website and its host a *takedown request* that asks sites to remove your content.

Before you start, reach out to someone for support like your sister, a very close friend, or—even better—a team. Think about who makes you feel protected, who in your life has reminded you that you're powerful, who makes you feel like who you really are, and who you'd pick to put on your own team of superheroes. Have someone who loves and supports you walk through the steps with you, because it's hard to stay organized when it feels like the Internet is your enemy. Have them present with you as you document and request content removal. Sure, you could do it alone, but it will help to have someone holding your hand—someone who knows and believes in you.

With your support system in place, start tracking down content for removal. Here are some tips:

- Make an evidence folder.

- List the locations of the private online content that you know about, including each website address and the "report abuse" or Digital Millennium Copyright Act (DMCA) information for the website. (You might find this information in the website's terms of service, its privacy policy, or a separate DMCA policy.)

- Take screenshots and download copies of the photos from each website; you're collecting evidence.

- Find more content using Google and its reverse image search. Use reverse image search to look for the photos you know are being used against you. In addition, image search your icon/avatar photos to see if they're being used without your consent anywhere else. To find this function, look in Google's search bar for the little gray camera icon, click it, and then follow the instructions.

- Do a regular Google search for image filenames, your phone number, the name and aliases of your harasser, and any other words or usernames associated with the images and posts.

- Take screenshots and download copies of the photos from the website.

- Create a Google alert for your name, your email address, and any unique names associated with the images or videos being posted about you (see "Eight Privacy Tips to Use Right Now" on page 4).

Make a document with all of the information you have about the person who's attacking you and posting your private images and information online. Now you can file your police report. But don't delete anything; you're still going to need it.

Next, start getting things taken down. Begin with a general removal request, even if you don't own the copyright to the image. Each website hosting the content will have its own form or contact procedure; again, look for the website's DMCA section. If you do own the copyright to the content and the website doesn't respond or won't take your images and videos down, you can submit an online copyright infringement claim form for each search engine (find forms at *http://copyright.gov/onlinesp/agenta.pdf*). Each search engine must give the person who posted the images a few days to file a counterclaim. But to file a counterclaim, they have to reveal their real identity.

You can also escalate to a DMCA takedown, under the right circumstances. First, use a site like *http://whoishosting this.com/* to learn who the website's host is. Contact each website's administrator and ask them to remove the videos or images. If you created the images or you own the rights to them, then you own the copyright, and you should ask for removal with a DMCA request. A DMCA request can be used when the images and videos are your original property, and an estimated 80 percent of private photos and videos that girls want removed is content they own. (Just be sure to only issue a takedown request if you own the copyright to the content.

If you misrepresent that you own the rights to an image or if anything else you say in your DMCA is incorrect, you can get in a lot of legal trouble—including a possible lawsuit under the DMCA.)

If you have a lawyer, run your DMCA takedown request by them. Some women use services like DMCA Defender, but make sure you read reviews or talk to others who have used these services before you trust them with your very private problem. You can find DMCA letter templates online, and there is one on page 147 of the Resources section.

Most websites with any adult content will have a DMCA-specific email address or a link for DMCA takedown requests in the Contact Us area of the website. When the website doesn't have one, send your takedown request via email to *abuse@<website>.com*, *DMCA@<website>.com*, and *admin@<website>*.com, and send a physical copy to any address you can find for the website. One of those email addresses or the snail mail address should reach a real person.

If You're a Minor

If you're a minor in your country (under the legal age of consent, which is 18 in the United States), you'll have an easier time getting naked or sexual photos and videos removed. When you follow the steps in this chapter for getting things taken down, make sure to tell them you're a minor. But if you're even a day older than the age of consent, don't claim to be a minor; if you're caught lying, the website owner might get angry with you and make things worse. And if you're pursuing legal action, misrepresenting yourself could count against you in other ways. (Ask your lawyer if anything like this comes up, because they can tell you what the laws are for the location you're taking legal action in.)

When you're a minor, a lot of social media sites will really rush to get your content offline. In some locations, you may have the law on your side for nonnude and nonsexual posts and photos, as long as they contain something that belongs to you. A 2015 law in California even states that websites and apps have to let people under 18 take their stuff down.

Outsourcing the Work

Another option is a *reputation service*. Reputation services find and address negative mentions of you online by deleting them or bumping them to somewhere they'll be less visible. The biggest business doing reputation cleanup is Reputation.com (formerly Reputation Defender). Again, be sure to read reviews of the service you're considering to see what its customers have to say before you sign up and hand over your money.

If you use a reputation service, make sure it's actually reputable. If the service is attached to, related to, or recommended by one of the sites where you've found private photos you didn't give someone permission to post, don't use it! It's probably a scam.

The cost of help from a reputation service varies a lot. It can be expensive if you have a stalker—or more than one stalker—who has been bothering you for a long time. For example, one man paid Reputation.com more than $10,000 to scrub hateful posts from his online footprint. (His girlfriend was the victim of online harassment, and when they started dating, her attacker started targeting him as well.) Yearly basic services for individuals start at around $5,000, and the company will make a plan to fit your situation. Remember that its goal is getting your money, though it does have systems, knowledge, access, and resources unavailable to you otherwise.

You'll notice that sites like Reputation.com do things that you can also do yourself, such as create positive content about you to push negative results off of top search pages.

(This is another reason not to delete your social profiles, and why you should be creating positive content about yourself, too.) But even huge companies like Reputation.com can only do so much, so don't expect any promises of "gone forever" to come true, because it's usually not 100 percent possible.

Still, for the guy who paid 10 grand to get rid of his girl-friend's stalker, Reputation.com managed to push the torrent of hate to page 27 of a Google search, and most search users don't go past the first page.

Also consider outsourcing tasks to freelancers around the world; they can do things you dread, often cheaply. For instance, you might use sites like Amazon's Mechanical Turk (*http://www.mturk.com/*), YourManInIndia.com, Remote Staff (*http://remotestaff.com.au/*), Elance.com, and so on to hire someone to check websites to make sure that content is removed. Just make sure to stipulate confidentiality and anonymity. Also, warn whomever you hire that there may be offensive content involved so they're not surprised.

Whether you use a reputation service, clean up the mess yourself, or hire freelancers, I suggest you still use the services of privacy companies such as Abine (*http://www.abine.com/*), which remove your private information from people-search websites. These services have already done the legwork, and they know their way around privacy-violating websites of all stripes and what websites are required to do under the law. Also, sites like Abine will go after privacy-violating websites until they comply.

Hiring a privacy company will probably also boost your mental health: it feels good knowing someone else is taking care of it, and you won't get bogged down or overwhelmed by frustration with the workload, or have to see all of that offensive stuff over and over again.

PREVENTATIVE MAINTENANCE

When managing your reputation online, create a system to manage all of the information you gather so you don't lose track of any important details. This will also leave you with an organized and complete file to hand over to your lawyer, law enforcement, a court, or any other authorities along the way.

A spreadsheet is a good tool for tracking the information. For example, if your attacker contacts you on the phone or harasses you on social media, add an item for that and a column for the date and time of harassment, in addition to screencapping and writing down everything. Sometimes your attacker's username or screen name will be a pseudonym (a fake name). Collect all of it, and you'll be able to spot patterns.

Here are some columns to add to your spreadsheet:

- Actions (anything your attacker has done, such as "posted photo," "posted video," "left comment," "made blog post," or "contacted me")

- The date the action happened

- The date you found out what the attacker had done

- Where the action took place (or the URL where it can be found)

- Any screen names or usernames associated with the posting, even if you know the attacker is using a pseudonym

- The name of the folder where you put copies and screencaps of the evidence

- Contact information for the website where the action took place, including its DMCA email address

- The date you sent a DMCA takedown notice

- The date the website responded and what the response was

Each situation is unique, and you might need to add columns for other information. For instance, if the website doesn't take your photo down and you decide to send a takedown notice to the website host, add the host's contact information, date of contact, and response.

Unfortunately, getting harassed, attacked, smeared, or worse online isn't the only damage an online privacy violation can do. What happens if someone uses your personal information to steal your identity? Read on, and I'll explain how to combat such a situation—and prevent it from happening in the first place.

"Sometimes you need to get hit in the head to realize that you're in a fight." —MICHAEL JORDAN

5. identity theft

Imagine that one day you wake up and find that someone has opened a credit card in your name and charged $10,000 to it. Or used your health insurance. Or maybe drained your bank account, hacked into your email and sent spam to everyone in your address book, and removed all your files in iCloud. Identity theft is a waking nightmare—and it becomes a real horror movie when you realize that some dude, somewhere, knows where you live.

Identity theft occurs when someone steals your personal information and uses it without your permission. They do this by collecting pieces of information about you from different sources and putting it together, like a dossier. Identity theft is a serious crime that can wreak havoc on your finances, credit history, and reputation, and it can take time, money, and patience to resolve. Once identity thieves have your personal information, they can drain your bank account, run up charges on your credit cards, open new utility accounts, get medical treatment on your health insurance . . . Basically, they can do anything you could do.

In this chapter, I'll show you how to deal with identity theft if it happens—specifically, how to quickly limit the damage and recover your life—and how to prevent it from happening in the first place.

Identity thieves are thinking about how to steal identities all the time, and they typically automate the technical parts, like sending out phishing emails. American and Eastern European crime syndicates are behind a lot of the world's identity theft, but there are a lot of small-time identity thieves, too. These small-timers use illicit software programs, but they also go through your garbage at home, survey your workplace, and haunt the town dump. They may work—or pretend to work—for legitimate companies, medical clinics, pharmacies, or government agencies and use that cover to convince you to reveal personal information. Some thieves contact you by email or phone, pretending to represent an institution you trust, and try to trick you into revealing personal information.

The good news is that more and more companies are aware of the problem of identity theft. Unlike the women who had to deal with this issue 10 years ago, at least you won't need to teach everyone you meet what the hell identity theft even is.

SIGNS OF IDENTITY THEFT

If you are a victim of identity theft, you will likely find out about it the hard way: you might get a letter from the IRS saying you have a tax problem, your credit card might max out when you haven't been using it much, or you may find that your bank account is empty the next time you write a check or try to use your debit card. Here are some things to look out for:

- Your credit card suddenly stops working or has weird charges.

- You can't withdraw your money from an ATM.

- Your bank statement shows withdrawals that aren't yours.

- You stop getting your bills or other important mail.

- A company or store tells you that your information has been compromised in a data breach.

- You receive emails about financial, medical, or shopping accounts you didn't set up.

- Your bank, credit card, or other financial service notifies you of a password reset that you didn't initiate.

- Your checks bounce, or a store suddenly won't take them.

- Debt collectors call you about debts that aren't yours.

- You find unfamiliar accounts or charges on your credit report.

- Doctors bill you for services you didn't use.

- Your health insurance tells you that you've reached your benefits limit, but you know you haven't.

- A health plan won't cover you because your medical records show a condition you don't have.

- The IRS tells you that multiple tax returns were filed in your name or that you owe taxes on income from a job you don't have.

Even if none of these signs is apparent, you should always be on alert. Keep an eye on your bank and other account statements for unusual activity. If you suspect that your wallet,

Social Security card, or other personal or financial information has been lost or stolen, act immediately.

RUN, DON'T WALK

If you suspect identity theft, take action immediately. Here's what you need to do:

- Freeze all compromised accounts.

- Place a fraud alert on your credit.

- Order your credit reports and note anything that is incorrect.

- Create an Identity Theft Report with the FTC (you'll need this to fix your credit reports and to dispute charges).

- Use your credit reports and your Identity Theft Report to fix your credit reports and get information about the thief.

- Call the appropriate authorities (like the IRS if your Social Security number has been compromised).

- Alert businesses involved in fraudulent charges.

Place a Fraud Alert

Placing a fraud alert is free, and it means that if the identity thief tries to open accounts in your name, the credit companies will call you. To place a fraud alert, call one of the three credit bureaus: Equifax, 1.800.525.6285; Experian, 1.888.397.3742; or TransUnion, 1.800.680.7289. (You only need to call one, because each is required to contact the others for you, but be sure to confirm that they will do so.) Tell the person on the phone that you are the victim of identity theft.

Mark your calendar for 90 days after the day you place a fraud alert. The alert lasts for 90 days, and you should renew it at least once.

Order Free Credit Reports

Once you've placed a fraud alert, you should be able to order free credit reports from the credit bureaus. Ask each company to show only the last four digits of your Social Security number on your report. When the reports come and you review them, check everything. You may well find unauthorized charges or accounts you didn't create.

File an Identity Theft Report

You'll find instructions for filing an Identity Theft Report on the FTC's website *http://consumer.ftc.gov/*, but you'll probably have to file the report at *http://ftccomplaintassistant.gov/*. Click **Identity Theft**, and then click the link that applies to you, such as Identity Theft: I am a victim of identity theft. Someone has used my personal information.

If you need help filing an Identity Theft Report, call the FTC at 1.877.IDTHEFT (1.877.438.4338). They should be able to answer your questions and connect you with the right law enforcement agencies. If the person who handles your call can't help you, hang up and try again. Maybe the next person can help. (This is a government agency after all.)

Contact the IRS

If you think someone has used your Social Security number to get a tax refund or land a job, or if you receive a notice from the IRS indicating a problem, contact the IRS Identity Protection Specialized Unit (1.800.908.4490). You should also submit IRS Form 14039, ID Theft Affidavit (*http://irs.gov/pub/irs-pdf/f14039.pdf*). Finally, alert the Social Security Administration fraud hotline at 1.800.269.0271.

Alert Businesses

If you know which accounts the thief has used, contact each affected business and jot down whom you contacted, when you contacted them, and the outcome of each contact. Speak with someone in the fraud department, and then follow up in writing, making sure to send correspondence by certified mail with a return receipt. And as you contact these businesses, request copies of any documents the identity thief used to open a new account or make charges in your name. According to the FTC website, "The business must send you free copies of the records within 30 days of getting your request. For example, if you dispute a debt on a credit card account you did not open, ask for a copy of the application and applicant's signature."

DON'T LET IT HAPPEN TO YOU

Identity theft can wreak havoc in your life, and not knowing who has your personal information or what they're doing with it can be really scary.

Sometimes when your identity is used without your consent, it will feel like your life has been violated. It has. If you're feeling scared, angry, confused, and overwhelmed, Chapter 4 offers tips on how to cope. But here are some tips to prevent identity theft from happening in the first place.

Prevent Identity Theft

These are some simple measures you can take to reduce the risk of your identity being stolen:

- **Prevention tip #1:** The minute you find out that a site or company you use has been hacked, change all passwords and information associated with your account, even if the hacked company tells you you're safe. Companies often don't inform the public of a security breach for a long time, and they often don't fully understand how badly they were hacked. And they lie.

- **Prevention tip #2:** Remove as much information as possible from people-finder websites: they're a gold mine for identity thieves and stalkers. Chapter 7 will tell you how.

- **Prevention tip #3:** Be stingy with personal information like your phone number, address, and everything in the red and yellow lists in Chapter 2.

- **Prevention tip #4:** Make sure that people aren't looking over your shoulder, or *shoulder surfing*, when you're on your phone or computer.

- **Prevention tip #5:** Don't let information used for security questions get out in the open. This includes things such as your pet's name, your mother's maiden name, your first car's model, the city you were born in, and so on.

Identity thieves don't like to work too hard, and it's often said that online criminals typically go after the low-hanging fruit (meaning the easiest things they can grab). Following these prevention tips will keep you safely out of reach.

Avoid Phishing Attacks

Phishing is a technique that criminals often use to attempt to steal your identity by tricking you into thinking that an email, SMS, or even a phone call is from an organization or company that you trust. Their goal is to dupe you into disclosing your personal information or login credentials when you connect to what appears to be a legitimate website or data collection form. Sometimes these sites or forms look surprisingly legitimate—like Facebook or Twitter; other times they're laughably bad. Some fake sites even display official-looking federal law enforcement symbols claiming to be, for example, the Federal Internet Enforcement Administration, and make bizarre threats designed to scare you into clicking their links or entering information!

To reduce your chances of becoming a phishing statistic, don't open files, click links, or download programs sent to you by strangers. For that matter, since a friend's email account may have been compromised, be wary when opening any attachment or clicking any link that you're not expecting or that just doesn't seem right. With malware attacks becoming increasingly sophisticated, almost any file you open—even an image file—could contaminate your computer with malicious software. Therefore, it's a good idea to make sure your email is set up to only display images from email addresses you have approved.

Security researcher Georgia Weidman writes:

> If you didn't order it and aren't expecting it, then you can be 99.9% sure it is a phishing attack. You can always contest any charges to your credit card if and when they show up. Ignore it. If you aren't the type of person who can ignore it, go to the company's website not by clicking a link but by typing in the web address you know and trust for that company.*

And let's not forget text messages sent to your phone. But it's just text, right? How can a text message compromise your phone? Clicking a link sent in a text can open a link in your mobile browser, which in turn can install password-stealing malware on your phone just as it might on your computer. Mobile browsers are no more immune to phishing attacks than your desktop browser is.

So if you get a text message that says you've won a $100 gift card to some store and you need to click a handy link to log in to claim your prize, don't do it. Once it's on your phone, the app can get access to any sensitive data stored on your phone, or it might run malicious code to get additional access. Bottom line: always question the source of incoming messages that invite you to respond.

---

* Georgia Weidman, "The Basics of Security Awareness Aren't Sinking In," Information Security Buzz, January 16, 2014, *http://www.informationsecuritybuzz.com/ georgia-weidman-basics-security-awareness-arent-sinking/*.

If Your Phone or Computer Is Stolen

The theft of a phone, tablet, or computer—or even just misplacing a device—puts your private information at risk, even if the device is protected by a password. When this happens, the first thing to do is change your passwords for the accounts that are connected to that piece of hardware. Use a friend's phone or computer if necessary, and get to work ASAP.

You don't necessarily have to change *all* of your key passwords, though. Think back to when you last used the device, and try to remember if you might have been logged in to your email, Facebook, Twitter app, or a shopping website (like Amazon). Make a list, change the passwords for these accounts immediately, and alert any credit card companies or other payment options (like PayPal) that might be connected to those accounts.

Install an Antitheft Tracking App

Unless your device is password protected or encrypted, or has an antitheft tracking app installed that lets you wipe or lock your device remotely, a thief may have access to everything you left open.

Tracking and antitheft apps allow you to track your devices remotely through an account on the app's website, and they give you a range of settings to activate when the device is lost or stolen. There are plenty of apps available to download, so choose the one that best suits you. Apple and Google both have their own antitheft apps, but others are available, too—check out Lookout, Kaspersky, McAfee, AVG, Where's My Droid, and Prey.

Prey is a great example of a tracking and antitheft app. It's free to download and super easy to set up. All good antitheft apps should allow you to activate them remotely and send you your device's location when it's not with you. The app should also offer a way to camouflage itself so a thief won't know it's an antitheft app. Prey disguises itself as a game, for example. You should have the option to remotely lock and wipe your device and have it ring, vibrate, or sound a siren on command, and you should be able to control these features easily by sending a text or by messaging the device through a web interface.

Your app should also be able to take photos from the device's camera and upload them to your online account so you'll not only be able to see where your laptop or phone is but who has it. Then you can give this information to the police.

Permanently Delete Information from Your Device

Computers, tablets, and phablets can all hold your personal and financial information, including your passwords, account numbers, addresses and phone numbers, contacts' addresses and phone numbers, medical information, tax returns, receipts, files left behind by browsers and operating systems, and much more. While all of that stuff is easy to save, it's tricky to make disappear, and sometimes that's exactly what you need to do. For instance, you might be selling your old laptop, upgrading your phone, or loaning a device out, and you want to make sure everything sensitive, like financial files, is wiped.

Unfortunately, even when you think you've deleted a file, it's not necessarily gone—bits and pieces of it remain on your computer, and they can often be retrieved with a data-recovery program. To remove data from a hard drive or your internal device memory permanently, you have to *wipe* it.

You'll find software tools to wipe hard drives online and wherever computers are sold. These programs are generally inexpensive, and some are even free. Some will erase the entire disk or drive, while others will allow you to select which files or folders to erase. Some overwrite or wipe the hard drive many times (the more wipes, the better), while others overwrite it only once.

Before you clean a drive, phablet, or phone memory, save any files you want to keep either online (to a service like Dropbox) or to an external hard drive or flash drive. Then use a program like Blancco (*http://dban.org/*) to wipe or overwrite the drive or the memory on your phone. If you're cleaning a phone, the phone should offer its own way to wipe or reset it, but don't forget to wipe the SD card too (or remove it entirely). And if you're wiping a phone, thoroughly check to make sure that your email, texts, photos, and personal files are really gone.

Finally, remove the SIM card, which might store your contacts, and the SD card, which contains files like your photos. Now your device is really wiped clean.

"If I could edit Google Images, then I wouldn't be as scared of the Internet." —CHLOË SEVIGNY

6. how to share

It's no secret that Yelp, Facebook, Google, and map apps know your current location, and you're probably cool with that because you want to use the services they provide in exchange. In fact, you're probably cool with sharing lots of information with these apps because they do useful things with it.

However, even if it weren't for Creepy Steve and your frenemies, social media can be used to hurt you if you're not careful about what you share. Anything you post on Twitter, Facebook, Google+, and other social media sites may be used to disqualify your job application or discipline you as an employee, and it can even be used as evidence in court.

Every social network and app is different, and social media companies change their privacy settings (and usage rules) all the time. That's why it's good to have a basic checklist at hand when you start using a new account or app and when you recheck its settings, which you should do often. This way, you pay attention to what you're sharing online and track those privacy policies.

But remember: anything you put online can potentially become public, no matter how tight your privacy controls are.

SOCIAL MEDIA CHECKLIST

Our relationship with social sharing—photos, videos, status updates, location check-ins, and more—changes as our lives evolve. The way we feel about sharing something one day may be totally different next week (or next year). At the same time, the companies we use for sharing change, too, and their privacy and sharing policies change with them, which sometimes leaves us exposed.

For all of these reasons, everyone should do a privacy check-up about every 90 days. Why every three months? Because companies like Facebook change their policies more often than that. Imagine if you opt to recheck your privacy only every six months: that would mean you're checking only twice a year. An embarrassing photo could be sitting out there on a public profile for half a year, and you wouldn't even know it.

Do this first: view your Facebook, LinkedIn, and Google+ profiles as someone else. Then adjust your privacy settings.

Don't panic if you see something you didn't realize was public, and don't blame yourself for what these companies have done to your privacy. What's online doesn't have to stay visible forever.

When you log back in to your account to adjust your privacy levels, review settings like these:

- Control your visibility
- What does my profile look like?
- What happens if I share my photos on other sites?

- Who can see my photos or location?
- How to remove my images
- How to delete my profile
- Tagging
- Personalization
- Location

Sharing Only What You Want

When you review what you've already shared, or if you're trying to decide what's safe to share before you press Upload or Share, consider the following:

- **Posting photos and videos:** When posting photos and videos, think about what you're doing in the image or video. Are you drinking with friends? Is your mouth wide open in an excited scream? Do you look exhausted or unkempt? Does the image reveal details about your home, work, credit card numbers, or vehicle? Is there a mailing address printed on an envelope?

- **Posting updates:** When posting updates to your online profiles, choose how you want to share that content every time, whether that's publicly, with friends, or only with certain people.

- **Posting comments:** When commenting on posts by others, pay attention to how you're posting. Are you posting with your real name? Does your comment reveal your name, location, or anything else that could be used to figure out private information?

- **Likes, upvotes, and favorites:** When you click Facebook's Like button, upvote a post, or favorite something, that action will be reflected in your profile. Then visitors to the item you favorited may see your picture and a link to your profile.

- **Friending:** When friending someone, ask yourself why you're friending them. Do you actually know them? Do you trust them with your personal information or with access to details about your friends and family?

- **The content of your posts:** When posting, never share anything on your red or yellow lists (like your entire birth date, address, or phone number) or news about a trip you're going to take (that you'll be away from home).

To reduce your online profile even further and for even better control of what you share, also consider doing the following:

- Select privacy levels for connecting with others on Facebook, including who can find you, who can send you friend requests and messages, and who can post on your wall.

- Edit the privacy settings for existing photo albums and videos to make sure that they're being shared only as publicly as you want them to be.

- Enable tag review.

- Disable settings like Suggest photos of me to friends and Friends can check me in to places. Settings that automatically share things for you in the background can often spring unwanted surprises, such as telling someone where you are (or worse, where you live!) when you'd rather have privacy, or sharing embarrassing or revealing photos without your knowledge.

Do a check-in on the privacy and sharing settings for all the apps and games on your phone, phablet, or tablet, too. A lot of apps have default settings that benefit the company that made them but make user privacy take a backseat.

One particularly problematic feature many apps have is instant personalization. This means that an outside company has partnered with a website to merge data sets. Both companies get access to data about you that they can monetize, and you get a combined and presumably more useful experience. For example, a site like Pandora would know your Facebook habits, and vice versa—and their advertisers would, too.

The biggest site to implement instant personalization has been Facebook, but other big social media sites have similar options in their settings. For example, Twitter's version of this is in Settings ▶ Personalization, with clear language that explains that you're letting Twitter track and record your activity outside of Twitter. So-called personalization is a clever way of making Facebook's advertising partnerships with Yelp, Pandora, and Microsoft seem like convenient features. And for a number of Facebook users, this is true—it's an easy way to integrate these services with their Facebook accounts.

But it's like having these sites spy on you wherever you go, and you don't have control over what they're sharing about you with each other. Options and settings that instantly personalize an app or service take away your control over your personal information, shopping habits, and other things you already have to fight to keep private. So turn them off, and don't fall for this attempt to trick you into trading privacy for convenience.

Friending

Online and approved friends have the most power over your private information, if you let them see it. If you wouldn't give an online friend the keys to your house, keep them locked out of your private life. And before you start friending anyone, find out how to block users and unfriend people.

Also, don't let anyone tag your posts without your permission. Review any check-in and tagging settings and be a tight-ass about it. The last time someone tagged you at a location and posted photos of you, they were sharing your location online.

BUT I CAN'T GIVE UP FACEBOOK
(OR INSTAGRAM, OR TWITTER,
OR FOURSQUARE, OR . . .)

It's estimated that nearly one quarter of the Internet's ads are run on Facebook. Advertising and data-mining companies are making billions *scraping* (collecting and analyzing) your personal data and selling it to any outside party that's interested. Companies that buy user information love Facebook because it has the most valuable vaults of data ever assembled: not only do you tell it everything you like, but it also knows what your friends like, which is an amazing predictor of what you'll like.

Social media sites do all they can to make sure the information they have about you is correct and complete, because it makes the information about you worth more money. They use your account data like your name, age, gender, email addresses, and location (information you enter when you sign up for services like Gmail, YouTube, Blogger, Picasa, and so on) to build your profile. Their many data trackers and ad agencies (like DoubleClick, AdSense, and AdMob) use the data stored on your computer and phone when you browse online, search Google Maps, or shop to learn more about you so that they can serve you better ads and make more money off you. Your information is freely bought and sold unless you squeeze your Facebook, Google, Yahoo!, and other privacy settings tight.

NOTE   *If you simply shut down a profile but don't delete it, it's actually still there on the site's computers. Unless you delete your information, companies can still use your info, even if you quit a site. If you're going to quit a site and never go back, always delete your profile—don't just disable it.*

Sometimes people online respond to concerns about social media sites and privacy by saying that we should "just quit" using Facebook (or other sites). But most businesses have social media profiles, so their employees need to have profiles on these sites, too. In other words, not using these sites simply isn't an option for people who want to be employed—or have a social life or stay connected to family. Fortunately, you can put limits on the information shared by social media sites. Here's how to do that with the two major ones: Facebook and Google+.

QUIT HUMPING MY LEG, FACEBOOK

Facebook is an awesome way to connect, but you need to make sure you don't share more than you mean to. Companies like Facebook are always trying to get more info about you to make your data more valuable to their advertisers, and they'll say anything to convince you to give up every little piece of personal information. Fight it at every step, because this sharing isn't for your safety or benefit—it's for their profits.

Because Facebook changes its privacy settings all the time, it's important to be more vigilant with Facebook than with most places you may hang out. Start by going to Facebook's Privacy Settings and Tools page (*http://facebook.com/settings/?tab=privacy*). As of this writing, you'll find three general sections: Who can see my stuff?, Who can contact me?, and Who can look me up?

Begin by reviewing the settings in each of these sections and carefully decide what you'd like to share and with whom:

- **Public:** What can people see on your profile? Check your public profile to see what's exposed to everyone. Most people only share a profile image, general location, and maybe school info or work history. It's a good idea to make anything else, especially photo albums and wall posts, available to friends only.

- **Friends:** From the same Preview My Profile Facebook page, you can type in any of your friends' names and see your profile exactly as they see it. This can help you manage what people on different lists can see.

- **Friend lists:** Is everyone on the right list? Double-check.

- **Photos:** Review all your photos and ones you're tagged in. Untag yourself and delete or ask to have any photos deleted that you aren't comfortable with.

- **Apps:** Facebook apps sometimes do sneaky, uncool things when you're not paying attention. Many spy on you and sell your habits to companies you don't know anything about. Get rid of the ones you're not using by looking in your account settings.

A Facebook account comes with numerous privacy violations, and you should fix them before you use Facebook even once. For one thing, Facebook will always ask you to add more information so that it can "connect you to friends," but you don't need to give up that information, ever. Don't let Facebook get more out of you than you want to give it. You can find your friends without telling Facebook more than it needs to know.

In fact, you don't need to have anything more in your Facebook profile than a name, an email address, a birthday, and a gender—and you can make it all up if you like. (You may even want to give Facebook a version of this personal information that is just for Facebook.) Everything else—like schools you've attended, your jobs, your current city, and your hometown—can stay blank. Facebook treats your name, photo, gender, username, and school and job information as public information, but only you should be able to decide if these things should be public.

First off, change Who can see my stuff? to **Friends**, not the dangerous default of Public. If you add things like Life Events to your timeline, they'll be public by default because you have to set the privacy level for each one. You get to decide who can send you friend requests or if you want your profile to be searchable, and you can set all these options to private if you like.

Furthermore, your choice of friends affects your privacy on Facebook, so choose your friends wisely. Set Review posts friends tag you in to **On** unless you want something embarrassing or too revealing to end up in front of everyone before you can stop it. Do the same for Review tags people add to your own posts.

Location Information in Photos

You can control whether or not your friends can tag you (telling Facebook and the public where you are in the process). If you don't want your location announced to the world, turn off tagging in Facebook's privacy settings.

The same goes for photo-sharing services like Flickr, Instagram, Imgur, and so on. You should find privacy settings in each that allow you to keep your photo's geolocation data to yourself. In Instagram, location is turned off by default, and you can remove location data in old photos.

Be Smart About Checking In

Be smart about checking in on Facebook, Foursquare, or any other app that tracks your location. Never check in at home, and never check in at someone's house or you'll just make it easy for a stalker to come find you right at that very moment in a private place. Also, never tag a photo with a location at someone's house unless the person whose house it is tells you that's okay. And don't forget to double-check your Fitbit or other personal tracker settings to make sure they're not broadcasting information to the world that you don't want Creepy Steve to know.

CONTROLLING WHAT YOU SHARE WITH GOOGLE AND GOOGLE+

Even if you haven't directly signed up for Google+, if you have an account with any Google site like YouTube, Blogger, or Gmail, you have a Google profile and a Google+ account because Google makes one for you. The Google Dashboard shows everything that Google says it knows about you, or at least the bits it will allow you to control. To view it, log in to a Google account and then go here: *http://google.com/dashboard/*.

Managing Your Google+ Profile

Now that you've taken a look at the Google Dashboard, let's go deeper into how to manage what you share in that Google+ profile that you didn't even know you had. Log in to Google+ by visiting *http://plus.google.com/*, and then work your way through the list below.

- **Google+ public profile:** To see what's made public in your Google+ profile, click **Profile** and change **View profile as** to **Public**.

- **Privacy settings:** You'll need to edit two sets of settings: your Google+ privacy settings and your (general) Google account privacy settings. To check your Google+ privacy settings, click your icon (in the upper-right corner) and then click **Privacy**.

    To see a menu of the general account privacy settings, sign in to your account and go to *http://myaccount.google.com/*. Read through each setting, and change anything you don't like.

- **Photos:** Check settings in *http://photos.google.com/*, *http://plus.google.com/*, and *http://picassaweb.google.com/settings/*.

- **Applications:** Go to *http://myaccount.google.com/* and review which services you've authorized to connect to your Google accounts.

- **Settings and services:** Finally, manage your overall Google+ settings at *http://plus.google.com/settings/*. (You'll find more useful information for managing and securing your account at *http://google.com/safetycenter/*.)

Locking Down the Privacy Settings on Your New Phone

Anytime you get a new phone from Verizon, AT&T, T-Mobile, Sprint, or any other major carrier, that phone will set its privacy settings in a way that makes your information most salable to advertisers. So every time you get a new phone, the first thing to do is to use a little privacy kung fu.

Don't let the clerk at the phone store set everything up for you lickety-split. You want control: slow them down so you can decide for yourself if you want Google or AT&T to know and report your location all the time. It just takes a second to interrupt them and tell them to let you see each screen and that you want to decide for yourself. It's also okay to ask them to tell you what each thing you say yes or no to means. If you can't get an answer you understand, that's a red flag: decline whatever the permission is until you know what you're agreeing to. You may not be able to complete the setup of your new phone if you decline some services, so make a note whenever a company won't let you opt out. That way, you'll know where the weak spots are in your privacy-protection armor so you can seal them up later.

When your phone gets an update with the latest firmware (the software that runs on the phone), set a PIN or password to prevent just anyone from unlocking it.

Be careful with the apps you install. Even apps from the largest companies or the most trusted app stores sometimes do really stupid and dangerous things with your privacy.

Additionally, many apps do things they don't need to do, like track your location or access to your contacts. Chances are, many apps on your phone—from dictionaries to games—are tracking your location without your knowledge.

Open your camera app, and make sure location reporting is turned off. Then open your social media apps (Facebook, Twitter, and so on), and make sure location sharing is off there, too. You don't want some creep to see where you live because you took your first photo with your brand-new phone at home.

Whenever you install a new app or update, instantly open that app's settings to see what you find. Look for items that are set to public, and make them private if possible. If you can't make them private, consider not using the app at all. And be sure to double-check any location and check-in settings. Don't let any app—or your friends—tell the world (or your friends) where you are unless you personally okay it each time. Otherwise, Creepy Steve will find out where you live.

SAFELY DISPOSING OF OLD DEVICES

In addition, be careful with what you throw away. Don't just toss your old phone, tablet, or computer in the trash. And never just hand it over to a reseller, trade-in outlet, or phone-for-cash service without wiping it. Remember from the last chapter that even if you delete everything, you leave behind all kinds of private account information. Wiping is the way to go.

Some people make a game out of finding people's information on discarded hard drives and devices; others make a living finding, selling, or otherwise using thrown-away (or traded-in) electronics to steal identities.

Scammers and identity thieves will go through trash for discarded devices, but it's not just dumpster divers who are scouring data off the phones and computers you throw away.

In 2014, a Sprint worker was caught sending around nude photos he'd recovered off a customer's phone—one a female customer had traded in for a new phone. That's why whenever you dispose of a computer or phone, it's crucial for you to scour all the personal information it stores.

What these scammers and creeps are doing is basically the same thing as a hard drive recovery. If you've ever had a computer, external hard drive, camera, or phone crash and die on you (or you dropped it and it stopped working), you probably know what a hard drive recovery is, because you paid someone to get your data back. Hard drive data recovery is possible because of *data remanence*, which means that some data still lives on a drive even after it has been "lost."

It's easy to make sure you get rid of your electronics safely. First, follow the instructions on how to save or transfer information to a new device. Transfer your phone book, lists of calls made and received, voicemails, messages sent and received, organizer folders, web search history, and photos. Make sure you've copied everything, because once you scrub your device, there's no going back.

Then, consult the service provider's website or the device manufacturer's website for the steps to delete information permanently. For a Mac, look on the Apple website for how to wipe the hard drive. For a Windows PC, you'll find a complete how-to on Microsoft's website.

Your phone already has built-in tools to securely erase the data on it. Each operating system is different, though. You'll go about wiping an iPhone differently than an Android or a Blackberry or a Windows phone. So google the steps for your exact device. In general, you'll look in the Settings menu for terms such as Erase all content and settings, Backup and reset, or Factory reset.

You're almost done! Some phone wipes are better than others, but no matter what type of phone you have, you need to remove your SIM card, because it's possible for contacts or call logs to still be on that card. If you have a micro SD card, don't forget to take that out, too. If you can't take the SD card out, you'll need to erase and format the SD card. You can find this function in your phone's settings.

"Ever get the feeling you've been cheated?"
—JOHN LYDON OF THE SEX PISTOLS

7. people-search websites

In February 2012, a man in Minneapolis stormed into a Target store with a fistful of coupons that had been sent to his house for pregnancy- and baby-related items. He was angry that Target was sending inappropriate mail to his house, where he lived with his teenage daughter.

Of course, the clerks at Target had no idea what he was talking about. But after going back home and talking to his daughter, he later apologized to the Target employees because it turned out that his daughter was, in fact, pregnant. Like most big companies, Target had created a profile of his daughter and tracked her, which is how it figured out that she was pregnant before her own father did.

Here's the deal. Every detail of your life—what you buy, where you go, whom you love—is being extracted from the Internet, bundled up, and sold by data-mining companies. That information comes from the websites you visit, the stuff you buy, your Facebook photos, your credit cards, your points and miles accounts, the music you listen to, the videos you watch online, the surveys you fill out, and the magazines you subscribe to. Add it all up, and you've got coupons about your supposedly private health status being sent to your home.

The sad truth is that when you visit Jezebel to read an article, you may think that only Jezebel is collecting your data. What you may not realize is that every ad on that page is also attaching a tracking code to you and collecting information about you.

BUT I'M NOT THAT INTERESTING

The information that you post on Facebook, no matter how boring or useless it seems to you, can make you a marketing target. Your bundle of information is sold to advertisers for about two-fifths of a cent as part of an enormous, multibillion-dollar industry that centers on the collection and sale of *you*. You are the product. And business is booming.

Shady data dealing has been around since the birth of junk mail, telemarketing, and credit companies, but the laws designed to keep us safe haven't kept pace with the Internet age. Tech-savvy businesses have realized that they can collect your data with abandon (even skimming it from apps on your phone that leak user data when they shouldn't).

Your personal and private info is worth more money when it's accurate. Unfortunately, many companies that buy and sell your information don't care about accuracy, as long as they can make even a little money off you as a product. Just as there are few legal safeguards to protect our privacy and our control over private information, the companies buying and selling your data also have not been held liable under any laws or accountable to any standards when it comes to protecting the security of your private information. They may share it to make money, or they may get hacked and your information may be stolen. This means your privacy is all up to you.

This can cause problems for you down the line in different ways, like wrong information ending up on your credit reports, or when you're dealing with identity theft. More and more, it can harm your reputation when wrong information is shared about you online, and it can harm your ability to get a job if a possible employer does an online lookup and gets bad information. The data dealers make plenty of mistakes, but I think the biggest one they've ever made is thinking that you don't care about your privacy.

Advertisers and ad brokers want to make sure they're getting their money's worth for their clients when they place ads on websites. They'll pay extra to have their ads seen by website visitors who are more likely to buy their clients' products. In some instances, the person being tracked on the website will be in a block of tracked people whose information is being auctioned off to the highest bidder.

In order to know whether a website visitor is likely to click on a diaper ad, for example, both the website owner and the advertiser want to have as much personal information as possible. They want to be sure a diaper ad is seen by the exact person who needs diapers at the exact moment they see the ad. This means that for online marketers, the more personal the information gets and the more accurate it is, the more valuable it is.

To aim ads at pregnant customers, Target gathers information from its baby shower registry and combines it with a website user's shopping habits and ordering information, like their address and phone number. The registry tells Target not only that a user is pregnant but also when her due date is.

If there's no registry, Target can still look at your shopping history to predict what's going on in your life. All of this adds up to a profile that is worth a lot of money, considering how much more Target can get people to spend if the company puts the right ads and coupons in front of them at the right time.

The same thing goes for ads placed on social media websites and other websites that make money off of selling targeted advertising. If Facebook figures out a user is pregnant, getting married, or any number of things we usually consider pretty personal, Facebook then takes some of the information it has on you and sells it to advertisers, who then buy ads on Facebook.

Some websites sell your contact information to advertisers and partners so those people can email you. Bottom line: if you want to keep personal things private, it's a good idea to read privacy policies before you sign up for anything. And if you do sign up—whether it's a mailing list, a shopper profile on a store's website, or a social media account—go into your account settings ASAP and make sure you're okay with what the company can and can't do with your information. Unfortunately, most companies limit the amount of your own information that you can control, and getting your info for free to sell later feeds their profits. Google is a prime example.

THE DANGERS LURKING IN PEOPLE-FINDER SITES

People-search services like Intelius, LexisNexis, Spokeo, WhitePages, BeenVerified, and DOBSearch get their information through public records, while secondary sites aggregate this information by data mining these sites. All of these sites are problems for your privacy. This is because they provide the general public with a dangerous amount of personal information about you. They offer to sell this information under the guise of promising to reunite lost family members or old friends, or providing detective services or phone book information.

With a quick search of your name on any given people-finder site, you'll most likely find your name, date of birth, names of family members, current and past addresses, phone number, and gender. Some sites will also reveal your marital status, hobbies, online profiles, and maps or a photo of your house. Intelius, for instance, claims to offer over 100 intelligence services, including a simple people search that provides a person's address and phone numbers and a background report showing criminal activity (though even Intelius conceded in a 2008 SEC filing that its information is often inaccurate and out-of-date).

Many people-finder sites will give up enough information about you for free to total strangers that finding out would make you choke on your latte. In other words, anyone with an Internet connection can stalk you from their couch with a couple dozen keystrokes.

Scary? Completely.

HOW PEOPLE-FINDER SITES GET YOUR INFORMATION

People-finder sites typically use these sources to compile their information about you:

- Birth certificates
- Business and entity filings
- Census statistics
- Criminal records
- Death certificates
- Driver's licenses
- Government spending reports
- Legislation minutes
- Marriage licenses and divorce decrees

- Political campaign contributions
- Professional and business licenses
- Real estate transactions (including appraisals)
- Sex offender registrations
- Trademark filings
- Unsealed lawsuits or legal actions
- Voter registrations

They also use information that you've supplied by doing any of these things:

- Completing surveys
- Entering sweepstakes
- Posting in forums
- Registering for online accounts and completing profiles
- Returning rebate and warranty cards

But don't throw in the towel yet. You can do something about this.

IT SOUNDS LIKE THERE'S NOTHING I CAN DO, SO WHY DO ANYTHING?

You can fight this crazy privacy invasion business by opting out of people-finder websites. (You'll find a sample opt-out letter and a list of websites to send it to in the Resources section.) The opt-out procedures are often complicated and daunting, and I'm pretty convinced that they're intentionally intimidating for the average person. That's because these sites don't want to remove your data. However, they'll usually do so if you officially request it, though you'll have to give them your information in order to get them to remove it. Something doesn't sound right there, for sure, but there's no other way to get the job done. Do what you can to block online tracking; it won't hurt to use browser add-ons that block targeted advertising cookies and trackers.

Many sites require that you scan and provide your ID, and they make things harder by accepting opt-out request letters only by fax or postal mail. If you need to send them your ID, *never* do so without blacking out your photo and ID number first.

Not only are the opt-out processes frustrating in general, but they are also all frustratingly different. While many of the companies are subsidiaries of the others, each has its own opt-out procedure, and some of the sites don't even state that opting out is possible in their openly stated privacy policies, even if they have backroom privacy policies that do allow it. Don't give up! This is still your information they're trying to peddle, and you can insist that they knock it off.

"I have guy friends, but the problem with having guy friends is, like, I always get linked to them, and they'll end up in a slideshow of people I've apparently dated on the Internet."
—Taylor Swift

8. dating and sexytime

Dating is stressful, but it gets an extra, heaping layer of stress with the worries that come with online privacy and security. From our own missteps (like if we accidentally share too much on Twitter) to companies putting our sensitive information online (as people-finder services do), dating is like a purse filled with candy and hand grenades. No girl wants to be freaking out about privacy when she's trying to meet someone to go out with, but it's important for you to manage your privacy when you're signing up for a dating site.

Most big dating websites have a page of privacy suggestions. Some are linked in really small print from the signup page, and others are buried within the site on a promotional blog post.

It's a good idea to read the privacy suggestions on each site you sign up for, but the sites may not make it obvious that you should read their advice before you make a profile.

Another problem with dating sites, and one that they aren't up-front about, is that a lot of them are fighting a serious problem with fraud.

Ever heard of the Nigerian bank scam or 419 scam? In a nutshell, it's targeted spam from an often fictitious someone who seems honest and who really seems to need your help. The scammer attempts to convince you that they know you or are somehow related to you in order to get you to send them money (or give them bank credentials). A lot of people fall for this scam over email, but now there's a big twist: these scammers are using dating websites to con single women out of money, plane tickets, and more. (It happens a lot on faith-based dating websites, where the thieves prey on a lonely lady's faith and goodwill.)

Aside from fine-tuning your bullshit detector, you can eliminate these scammers like cockroaches by following some simple privacy rules, as explained in the next section. Don't sign up for a dating site until you read these rules—they'll help you keep creepers from getting any power or control over you, too.

MAKE A SMART DATING PROFILE

The key to a bulletproof dating profile is making sure that you control how much can be found out about you—both what real (and private) information people get to learn about you and when they get to learn it. It's easy to make a safe profile if you take the right precautions.

For one thing, never put your personal contact details in your profile—that means nothing from your red or yellow alert lists in Chapter 2. Always make up a fake birth date and use a screen name (or nickname) that isn't your first and last name, because you can be tracked when someone discovers your real name.

Never use your real email address (or your work email address!) on a dating website. Use a free email account and make sure to use your dating website screen name or another nickname in the "from" and signup fields. This protects you from anyone trying to search your email address to find out more about you on Google, on social websites, or anywhere else your email address can be found online.

Pay attention to your photos: use photos on your dating profiles that aren't used anywhere else, unless you want people to be able to easily find out who you are and what you do (or more). Google and a few other websites allow anyone to search images. All you have to do is upload a photo, and the search engine will show you all copies of the image that can be publicly found, with links to the sites where the photo is located. Before you add photos to your dating profile, use Google's Search by image to make sure your images won't reveal things you're being careful to keep private. Your best bet is to always take separate photos for your dating profile.

Keep everything on your red and yellow list private until you're ready to share it and you know the person you're sharing it with is safe. Always keep your personal information private during the initial stages of dating. If you choose to share your computer with others, disable the auto sign-in feature on your account, clear your history after you check the dating site, and clear all saved passwords so you won't accidentally expose your dating profile to someone who shouldn't be seeing it.

Don't add a potential date or even a current dating partner to your Facebook, Instagram, or other social media site until you're sure they're safe. This may sound harsh, but it's a terrible idea to do so until you know the person better. Your photos, your profile info, and even your friends and family will give away much too much about you, and sometimes it can take a few months before you realize you've let a stalker into your social media (or your real) life. You don't want to find out that your potential date's real name is Creepy Steve after he's made himself Facebook friends with your coworkers, your besties, or your mom.

SCREEN OUT SCAMMERS AND STALKERS

The US Federal Trade Commission has solid advice for screening out scammers and stalkers. Cut off communication with, don't trust, and give a big fat boot to the ass of anyone who does any of these things:

- Asks for your real name, location, address, workplace, schedule, phone number, real email address (or anything else on your red and yellow alert lists).

- Asks too quickly to talk or chat using an outside email or messaging service.

- Claims to be from the United States but is currently traveling, living, or working abroad, especially if they say they're in trouble and need your help. (Some scammers claim they've been stabbed and robbed and are in an overseas hospital.)

- Asks for money.

- Vanishes mysteriously from the site and then reappears under a different name.

- Talks about "destiny" or "fate."

- Claims to be recently widowed.

- Asks for your home, workplace, or school address under the guise of sending flowers, presents, or gifts.

- Asks for pictures of you in front of your house, your work, or near a vehicle with your license plate visible.

- Makes an inordinate number of grammar and/or spelling errors.

- Sends you emails containing strange links to third-party websites.

If something just doesn't add up about someone you meet online, hit the eject button. Don't start revealing personal information until you've checked someone out completely and they haven't raised even one red flag.

Finally, don't even begin to plan a meeting until you read the safety guidelines at Chemistry.com (*http://chemistry .com/help/safety/*). They explain how to prepare for talking about a first meeting and how to meet safely.

MAKE THE INTERNET WEAR A CONDOM

No one wants to be watched online, but if you don't check a couple of settings and add some quick and easy apps to your browser, you will be. You'll be surprised at how easy it is to keep your computer from being clogged with trackers, which report your surfing habits to marketing agencies or record your (sometimes embarrassing) search history in the profile these companies keep on you. You don't want someone secretly intercepting your Internet connection in a café and snooping on you or, worse, spying on you and stealing your stuff.

When you go online to visit websites, you'll be using a web browser like Firefox, Chrome, Internet Explorer, Safari, Opera, or Dolphin or your phone's Internet app. Each has different levels of privacy protections, and you can amp them up with various extensions and add-ons. The two browsers considered at the top of their game for privacy are Firefox and Chrome.

As a first step, visit the website for your browser and download and install any security patches or updates (follow the directions there). Microsoft's Internet Explorer is the most vulnerable, but you can set your browser preferences to automatically check for new security and virus patches daily—which you'll especially want to do if you're on a PC rather than a Mac, regardless of your browser. Computers running Windows are more vulnerable to attacks, viruses, and malware than Apple computers, but no computer is completely safe. Run all the security updates your computer tells you to, and check for browser updates monthly. Make it a habit, like brushing your teeth.

Not many people know this, but an important part of Chrome's security safeguarding expires if it doesn't get its once-a-month update. Click the Chrome menu on the browser toolbar and select **About Google Chrome**. Chrome will check for updates when you're on this page. Click **Relaunch**, and you're all set.

While you're doing privacy chores, schedule a virus scan to make sure that no cybercrime rings put a malware/spying program on your hard drive that time you accidentally opened an attachment you thought was from a friend.

Evil comes in the form of sites or files you download (whether on purpose or together with something else that you download) that install malware, spyware, or viruses designed to infect your computer. Malware can even be injected into your computer just from you visiting a site (called a *drive-by download*). Spyware, malware, and viruses can send private information about your online browsing and search habits to a puppet master controlling them. The mess must be cleaned up with an antivirus program or malware remover.

PRIVATE TIME ONLINE: BROWSING PRIVATELY AND SECURING YOUR SENSITIVE INFORMATION

What you do in your private time should be nobody's business but your own—even if that means looking at adult content online; doing embarrassing searches; researching health problems; downloading a friend's private photo or a file to your hard drive; or finding answers about love, sex, and relationships. Or maybe you share a computer at home, and you just want some privacy when you check Facebook. There is no bad reason for keeping things private.

Privacy keeps us sane and emotionally strong. You're not doing anything wrong when you want to erase your tracks both online and offline.

One way to protect your privacy online is to use a *VPN*, or *virtual private network*, to mask your computer's IP address. You can use a VPN to secure access to your own network as well as to public Wi-Fi or Internet access spots. It's a great way to keep your browsing private and attack-proof.

The easiest way to set up a VPN is to subscribe to a VPN service, and there are a lot of great inexpensive ones to choose from. (You'll learn more about using a VPN in Chapter 9, "Ninja Tricks.") A VPN is also a handy way to protect your identity if you want to leave a comment or browse secretly without the website you're visiting knowing your location.

Search Engine Creep

Did you know that search engines (like Google) can track your searches, the information your computer sends them, and more? Some of these you can control in a search engine's settings (though it will require you to make an account to opt out of some tracking), but some search engine snooping you can't stop. Your personal information can be revealed when you search online (especially when you're logged in to an account like Facebook, Google, or Twitter), because your IP address (your computer's address online) can be linked to the search terms you've used (the better to serve you targeted ads). Unless you use a VPN to keep your IP address private, search engines can also use your IP address to find wherever you are in the world. Google, Facebook, Twitter, Instagram, and all of your favorite social media sites make money by tracking you, packaging you up as a product, and selling your information to advertisers. Search engines can retain your information, such as your current location and the time you spend using the search engine, for up to 90 days.

Cookies

You've probably heard the word *cookies* bandied about or seen it pop up on a site with a note about using third-party cookies. Cookies are pieces of information stored on your computer when you visit websites. These cookies send information back to the websites and the companies that place them. Sometimes they're only on your computer temporarily; other times they're there indefinitely (unless you delete them).

In many cases, cookies are useful and no big deal when their only job is to remember you on a site where you want to remain logged in. They might unobtrusively send your password and user ID to a site so you don't have to log in every time you leave and come back. (Many people find this very helpful, but remember to log out if you leave your computer unattended. And keep in mind that when you're logged in on a site like Facebook, its cookies can still track you even when you're not using the site.)

But most third-party cookies are used for *data-mining* purposes. They're there to track you and build the cookie owner's dossier on you. Some companies even participate in cookie-sharing rings. They share (sell) your info to hundreds or thousands of data buyers. They don't ask for your permission, they are probably getting some embarrassing stuff, and the only way to stop them is to tell your browser to not allow third-party cookies and to occasionally clean out your browser's cookies, history, and cache.

Leave No Trace

To keep your information and interests private, after you surf the Internet, clear your browser's *history* (the record of where you've been online), *cache* (a repository for stored data about sites you've visited), and cookies. You may not be able to do this on a work or school computer, so that's a good reason not to do anything private at work or school. And if you walk away from your computer in a public space, even just to go to the bathroom, log out of everything you're using and lock it.

Browsers have different stealth modes that you can use for private browsing, as long as you remember that they don't completely cover your tracks. Firefox allows you to open a New Private Window from its menu, but it's not completely private. When you open a private window, Firefox won't record your browsing history, but you'll notice that you're still logged in on some sites. Chrome's Incognito Mode is similar. But none of the stealth modes will make you anonymous online.

Keep Your Sensitive Files Private

Anything you print can usually be traced to you if someone has enough money, time, and motivation to find you. If you're worried about printing certain files, put them on a USB stick (super cheap on Amazon) and take them to a copy shop. Carry the USB stick with you, and password protect it if possible.

Erase Files Completely

When you delete a file simply by pressing DELETE on your keyboard or dumping it in the Trash or Recycle Bin, it's not really deleted. Unless you obliterate the file using specialized software, it can be recovered simply by undeleting it or doing a disk recovery. The disk recovery may not be cheap and it may take time, but money and time aren't enough to prevent motivated people from pursuing something that they want badly.

You would be amazed at the sensitive information people throw away with their computers every day. A hacker at an underground hacker conference in San Francisco gave an entire talk (with a slideshow) of what he found by doing data recovery on hard drives he bought off of eBay. The highlight of his March 2014 demonstration was showing the sensitive information he recovered on the hard drive that belonged to a guy who runs a service wiping and selling hard drives.

When deleting files, choose a Secure empty trash option if it's available, even if that takes a long time. If you're really worried, use a program that securely wipes (not deletes) your sensitive data.

Make Your Browser Private

One of the key steps in making sure that your sensitive information remains private and secure is to reduce the information that your web browser shares. First, go into your browser's settings and take a look at the privacy and security bits. Turn off anything that clearly says it's tracking you: for instance, Firefox has a little button you can click that says, "Tell sites that I do not want to be tracked."

Here's how to access the privacy and security settings from each browser menu:

- **Chrome:** Settings ▶ (Show advanced settings) Privacy

- **Firefox:** Preferences ▶ Privacy

- **Internet Explorer:** Tools ▶ Internet Options ▶ Privacy

- **Safari:** Preferences ▶ Privacy (and Preferences ▶ Security)

- **Safari mobile:** Settings ▶ Safari ▶ Privacy & Security

Once you're in these menus, you can tinker with the settings. Don't sweat it if you don't understand a lot of what you see. Remember, if you change a setting that causes a behavior you don't like, it's a snap to change it right back. Here are the primary things to adjust:

- **How the browser handles your history:** Do you want it to save a list of the pages you've visited online? If not, make sure you clear your browsing data.

- **The files you've downloaded:** If you don't want a list of files you downloaded hanging around, change this setting (you'll still be able to download files—the browser just won't keep a record).

- **Information you enter into forms:** It's convenient to have our email address, home address, or name automatically filled in on a form, but that means anyone can see this information if they use your computer. Turn this off.

- **Cookies:** You can choose which sites can give you cookies and which cookies to remove from your browser to prevent sites from tracking you. For instance, if I visit a Facebook page, I always clean the cookies out afterward so Facebook can't keep tracking me. Blocking cookies can make some websites impossible to use, which is annoying, so experiment with your cookies settings to see what keeps you safe and sane at the same time.

Do Not Track

With Safari mobile, you can turn on antiphishing, and with all of these browsers, you can change a preference that tells the browser you don't want to be tracked by websites. For instance, in Chrome, you can include a Do Not Track request with your browsing traffic, and with Firefox, you can turn on the setting Tell sites that I do not want to be tracked. The Do Not Track setting is really only a suggestion from the browser, and it's ignored by websites that don't choose to respect it. Still, it can help, so always activate it. (Turning on this setting shouldn't affect your browsing experience otherwise.)

Private Browsing

You should find a Private Browsing setting in every browser (Chrome calls it Incognito Mode). You should be able to set private browsing to On in Settings (or Preferences) or use it on a case-by-case basis by simply opening a separate browser window from the drop-down menu under File.

The term *private browsing* fools some people into thinking it makes their online activity anonymous—it doesn't. Websites can still see the identifying information coming from your computer or mobile device, such as your IP address and your browser's unique identifiers. What private browsing actually does is force the browser not to save your history or any form information—read: no autocomplete, no saved passwords, no saved Downloads list, no temporary (cached) content, and no cookies.

There are thousands of excellent Firefox extensions, Chrome plug-ins, Safari add-ons and extensions, and IE add-ons for privacy protection, but there are also a lot of bad, fake ones, too. (Browser extensions, plug-ins, and add-ons are apps that you can use to customize your browser in a bunch of different ways.) But don't add them all or you could slow down the browser a lot.

When choosing extensions, read reviews, look at what's popular for privacy and security, and choose wisely. It's usually okay to trust plug-ins and extensions that come from reputable companies and developers, but if you're concerned, search for them online to see if users are complaining about something. I recommend installing these plug-ins and extensions to turn your browser into a privacy shield:

- **AdBlock Plus:** Blocks ads and tracking for most advertisers.

- **AVG PrivacyFix:** Manages all social media privacy settings.

- **Blur:** Blocks tracking, manages passwords, offers disposable email addresses, and much more.

- **BugMeNot:** Bypasses the sign-in on websites that require your info to simply read a page.

- **Cocoon:** Blocks tracking and offers disposable email addresses.

- **Disconnect:** Blocks Facebook tracking.

- **DuckDuckGo:** A nontracking search engine

- **Ghostery:** Alerts you to bugs, tracking, and ad networks on sites you visit. It can be overwhelming and controversially resells anonymized user metrics.

- **HTTPS Everywhere:** Enables encryption automatically on sites that support it.

HOW TO TELL IF SOMEONE WAS ON YOUR COMPUTER

If the idea of someone physically looking through your computer when you're not around makes you feel like (a) someone just dug through your underwear drawer and (b) you want to Hulk-smash something, then welcome to the None of Your Business club. You should be mad, and yes, it's a total violation. The person who looked through your life either knew they were doing something wrong or thinks it's their right to go through your stuff. Both of these are never okay.

If someone pokes around on your computer when they know they shouldn't, they're usually looking for something they don't have permission to look at. They may think you are cheating on them, lying, or worse. Whatever the reason, it's wrong. They should just come out and ask you or live with the fact that it's none of their business.

When someone in your life invades your privacy, they may think they're protecting you or otherwise doing it "for your own good." But it's up to you to decide what's good for you.

If they want to warn you about something or they're worried about a serious risk to you, the first thing they should do is talk to you, not snoop on your computer. Parents and older family members sometimes think that spying on you is the best way to make sure you're safe, but that approach always backfires. It makes you not trust them, it makes you figure out how to have your own privacy anyway, and whatever it is they want to protect you from is always something they should talk to you about, in person.

A longtime friend of mine is a computer-savvy dad, and he's really cool with his daughter—about talking about sex, having her ask about anything, explaining scary stuff, and letting her evaluate her own risks and feelings. Sometime after she turned 14, she and I were hanging out while her dad went to get coffee. I asked if her dad made her use Internet filters or share her passwords, and she said yes.

I heard all about the Internet filters at home, how all of her social media accounts were password shared with mom and dad, and how a lot of things around the house were password protected and everyone had their own login accounts. It sounded like her high-tech dad didn't give her much privacy, and I asked if she thought it was weird. She told me no, because her dad was cool and she didn't care if he checked in on her, but she could tell he hardly ever did. Besides, she told me, "And don't tell my dad, but I cracked our house passwords a long time ago, and I have separate social media and email accounts he doesn't know about under different names. I clear everything all the time. Everyone at school has different names online."

She knew she was being spied on, and it was just her dad and mom, but they were honest with her about being big old snoops. It may not have seemed fair, but she had an expectation that under the family roof, her parents were watching her online and they didn't do it behind her back.

When someone tries to spy on your computer without telling you, there are some simple ways to find out.

- Look at the Most Recently Used items on Windows or at Recent Items from the Apple menu on a Mac. You'll see your recently used applications, documents, and servers. Open your web browser and look at the history and cookies.

- Type letters in alphabetical order into the URL (address) bar, search bar, and search engines to see what comes up—this works if any kind of auto fill is turned on, which is usually on by default.

- Check the Trash or Recycle Bin on your Desktop for files that may have been deleted by someone digging around and trying to hide their tracks—or see if the Trash is empty when you know you didn't leave it that way.

- If you decide to restore any files you find, make sure you note where the file's original location was, because that's where the file will reappear after you undelete it.

- You can also install monitoring software like a keylogger to secretly record what anyone types when they use your computer.

"I think it's better to have your personal life and your work life separate. That way they don't corrupt each other, so to speak."
—ZOOEY DESCHANEL

9. ninja tricks

You don't have to be a hacker to use advanced tricks and techniques to secure your data and lock your privacy down tighter than the average person does. There's quite a bit of privacy and security kung fu you can do to protect yourself that doesn't require technical acumen (though if you want to get technical, there are plenty of options for you to take your privacy and security as far as possible).

One of the things repeated in information-security circles is that people don't want to sacrifice convenience for security, and this is the source of many headaches for companies that want to make things more secure without making something like a sign-in process annoying for users or customers. While it may be true that convenience will trump security most of the time for the average person, adding a layer of security to your credit cards or bank accounts will make any inconvenience seem like a fine trade-off in the event your account information gets into the wrong hands.

NINJA YOUR CREDIT CARDS

We've learned the hard way that even the biggest companies are vulnerable. It's estimated that over one million people a year are victims of identity theft. Credit card account information theft and fraudulent charges are becoming more common, and credit card companies are struggling to combat the increasing number of charges they have to swallow for customers whose accounts have been compromised.

While you're not legally liable for fraudulent charges over $50 (per transaction) in the United States, companies are starting to make it harder for account holders, especially ones who are repeatedly victimized. For instance, credit card companies can make you go through the process of making a statement under oath in order to contest charges you didn't make. In some cases where an account is compromised more than once, the bank may also make you go through an arduous process to prove your identity (including taking your Social Security card to a local branch of the card issuer's bank in person). And if you don't do as asked, the bank will simply close your credit card account(s)—immediately, even if the theft wasn't your fault.

So even though this is actually a problem with the way these institutions are dealing with security and consumer protection, the responsibility is on us to protect our credit cards more than ever. Here's what to do to tighten the defenses on your credit cards and limit your risk if they're lost or stolen:

- Use prepaid credit cards or gift cards when shopping. You can use your regular cards most of the time and use gift cards when you don't trust where you're shopping to lessen your chances of ending up on a victim list. If you lose a gift card or someone steals it, you aren't at risk for losing any more than the value of the card. (You'll find a list of prepaid credit cards in the Resources section.)

- Try one-time use, disposable credit cards. Ask your bank or credit card company if it offers them. While not the most convenient way to shop, these disposable card numbers typically have a 24-hour use window or limit your purchases to a fixed amount, so even if the number is stolen, a thief can't do a lot of damage. Another service worth considering is called a Masked Card. MaskMe (*https://www.abine.com/maskme/*) allows you to create unique, disposable credit cards in specific amounts; they're like prepaid gift cards that you can create as you shop. The charge shows up on your credit card bill as "Abine Inc.," so the shop never receives your real credit card information. If the store gets attacked, your credit card is still safe, and Abine doesn't store your credit card information, either.

NINJA MOVE: FREEZE YOUR CREDIT

Not many people know that they can place a security freeze on their credit. It's one of the top ways to prevent identity theft, but the companies that manage your credit scores (Experian, TransUnion, and Equifax) won't be running Super Bowl commercials about security freezes anytime soon because when you freeze your credit, you severely limit their ability to sell your information.

In every US state, a credit freeze effectively stops all access to your credit report and blocks the process of issuing new credit. You have to unfreeze your reports when you want to apply for credit, like a new credit card, a loan, or anything else that requires a business to check your credit. You can lift the freeze temporarily for an amount of time that you specify, or you can have it completely lifted.

Placing a security freeze is an incredibly smart thing to do. Once you've frozen your credit, no one can pull your credit report without your permission, and if a thief tries to do something like open a credit card in your name, you'll find out and the criminal will be blocked. A security freeze is different from a fraud alert (which you should place if a company you do business with was breached—see Chapter 3).

It's not free: it usually costs around $10 (and you have to do it at each credit agency's website—Experian, TransUnion, and Equifax—who don't make it easy). It will cost you another $10 to lift the freeze, which is what you'll do when you apply for credit cards or loans in the future.

Here's where to go to put a credit freeze in place:

- **Experian:** *http://experian.com/freeze/center.html*
- **TransUnion:** *http://transunion.com/securityfreeze/*
- **Equifax:** *https://www.freeze.equifax.com/*

Here are the links you'll need to set fraud alerts:

- **Experian:** *http://experian.com/fraud/center.html*
- **TransUnion:** *http://fraud.transunion.com/*
- **Equifax:** *https://www.alerts.equifax.com/*

STEALTH OUT YOUR MAILING ADDRESS

People do evil things all the time. Websites and online apps are attacked. Creeps steal our purses and keep our ID cards. One way to protect yourself and your privacy is to set up a mailing address that's different from your home address. This is one that you can use with social media websites and apps and even attach to your credit cards.

Another way is to rent a mailbox at the local post office or a place like a UPS Store licensed to rent them, and then use your box to receive mail that you don't want coming to your house. Although federal law in the United States doesn't allow you to use a PO box or mail center address to apply for bank accounts or credit cards, once you have the account set up, it's perfectly legal to change your mailing address to your PO box mailing address. This way, when you use your credit card somewhere dodgy and have to enter an address associated with the card, you won't be handing over your home address.

You should also use your mailbox address for things like your cell phone bill and website registration or even when paying total strangers by check: use the checking account that has your mailing address attached and never your home address.

STEALTH OUT YOUR PHONE NUMBER

To prevent your phone number from being spread around where you don't want it to be, set up a second phone number that forwards to your main number. If you have a land line at home, you might make a cell phone number that second number, but a better option would be to get a free phone number online, which you can then either access only online or forward to your main number only when you want to.

You can set up a second phone number using popular services like Skype (very cheap) and Google Voice (free). Another option is to use disposable masking phone number services, like Burnerapp.com, which will let you create a temporary phone number to use and then delete it forever.

NINJA TRICKS:
ENCRYPT YOUR PRIVATE COMMUNICATION

When former government contractor Edward Snowden leaked documents to the press revealing widespread surveillance by the National Security Agency (NSA), we learned that—for better or for worse—governments can spy on anything they want to. And when government authorities fail, they make private companies hand over information about users. The people being spied on never know the difference. In fact, companies like Google, Yahoo!, Microsoft, and others have been very public about the fact that this happens every day.

The people who work at companies like Google, Microsoft, and Facebook and agencies like the NSA also do bad things for their own purposes all the time. In 2010, Google fired an engineer who cyberstalked and spied on the Gmail and Google Voice accounts of several teens. He was the second Google employee to be publicly fired for spying on Google users. In 2013, US officials confirmed to the *Wall Street Journal* that NSA officers and employees were known to use the agency's eavesdropping tools to spy on spouses, love interests, and more—so much so that the practice has a nickname like one of the NSA's spy operations—LOVEINT, short for love interest.

It's all enough to make a girl really want to have truly private communication. You can protect your email, instant messaging, texting, and Internet browsing from most attacks like these. Here's how.

Protecting Your Email

The only way to truly, 100 percent keep your email private is to use OpenPGP email encryption, which protects your email so that the only person who can read it is the one you're sending it to. (*PGP* stands for "pretty good privacy.") With free services such as Mailvelope, any recipient you send an encrypted message to will have to enter a password to read it—and without the password, your message will just look like a bunch of garbage. Gmail/Google Apps, Outlook, Yahoo!, and GMX are all supported, and the app can be configured to support others.

Mailvelope is a browser extension for Google, Chrome, and Firefox that allows secure email communication based on the OpenPGP encryption standard. The framework of Mailvelope and products like it is relatively straightforward. First, install the plug-in. Next, you'll generate a key pair, which means you'll use the plug-in to make two sets of code. One set is called your public key, and this is the one you'll publish. Each contact in your address book who uses PGP or products like Mailvelope will have their own public key, too.

The next time you open Gmail, Yahoo!, or whichever email brand you use, you should notice a lock icon in the compose area when you begin an email. When you're done writing and ready to send, just click on the lock icon, and Mailvelope should encrypt the message with the recipient's public key (if they have one) when you hit send.

When you get an email that's encrypted, the process goes in reverse. You should see the encrypted message with a lock on it, so just click it to enter your key as a password to open it. Mailvelope will then search your saved keys to find the right one and decrypt the message for you.

You can purchase commercial PGP software or use plug-ins like Mailvelope, or if you're technically inclined, download the open source version that uses the OpenPGP protocol, such as GPG (GNU Privacy Guard). No matter what, if you want to send an encrypted email, you need your recipient's public key (if they have one).

NOTE   *Many PGP implementations have plug-ins for different email clients, such as Outlook on PCs or Mail on Apple computers. As with all software, this can be problematic when system updates and PGP implementation updates don't come at the same time. Also, it's important to note that you might be restricted from using PGP at work or on your employer's network.*

Keeping Your Chats Private

The best way to keep your online messaging secure is to use a tool called Off-the-Record (OTR) messaging. OTR encrypts your instant messages when you use services like Google Hangouts and Facebook Chat. Chat/IM software clients like Adium, Xabber, TextSecure, and ChatSecure all come with OTR messaging, and there are OTR plug-ins you can get if you use clients like Pidgin. OTR encrypts your messages so they can't be read if someone intercepts them, but it doesn't let you save your chats—which might be a desirable thing, depending on how private you want to make your communication. Using OTR means that even the service sending and receiving your IMs and chat can't read the content.

Although it's the best tool we have today, PGP encryption (and OTR) isn't perfect. If the NSA really wants to spy on you, it will figure out a way to break OTR (if it hasn't already). It's important to also consider that there are ways for people interested in digging up dirt on you to use information that PGP doesn't encrypt to find out the recipient of your message, when you messaged them, their IP address, and so on. But unless you're hiding state secrets or doing something really nefarious that will make the authorities hunt you down, PGP and OTR should do the job for you, because you probably care more about keeping your messages confidential than about evading authorities. That said, if you're a female activist (or journalist, blogger, or writer) in a country where you're a government target, use encrypted communications with caution: reports of activists "flagged" for targeting because they use encryption (or privacy tools such as Tor) are not uncommon.

Encrypting Your Internet Activity

You've probably noticed that some websites you visit have *http://* while others have *https://* at the beginning of the URL. The difference is the *s*, which stands for—you guessed it—*security*. The *s* means that the site you're visiting is using encryption as a secure layer for the sending and receiving of your information. So if you fill out a form, press Submit, and the website doesn't have the *s*, it means that attackers could read all the information you just submitted to the website. If instead the website is using *https*, the information being sent over the Internet is encrypted, and it can't be read by anyone snooping on Wi-Fi—or any network—traffic. Needless to say, you should never ever enter your credit card number or any information from your red list into a website that only uses *http*.

There's a huge push by security professionals to get all websites to use *https*. Unfortunately, adoption has been slow, and a lot of big companies that transmit sensitive information may still not use it. Until these companies come around to using *https*, you can use the Electronic Frontier Foundation's HTTPS Everywhere browser add-on for Chrome or Firefox to maximize the amount of web data you protect by forcing websites to encrypt their pages when you visit them, whenever possible.

NINJA CHOKE HOLD: STRONG, EASY PRIVACY APPS

Privacy and security protection apps are a growing business arena, and like all sectors, it's a "buyer beware" area of technology. While it's great that so many privacy and security products are hitting the market for consumers, it's important to remember that if something seems too good to be true, it probably is. Yet the emerging technologies that are from reputable sources are really exciting, and they're all making it much easier for us to protect our privacy from both malicious attackers and greedy companies who like to snoop.

There are a lot of hackers fighting the good fight for privacy, and some have even created apps that make some pretty hardcore privacy work easy. These highly recommended ultra-privacy apps include TextSecure (text messages), ChatSecure (IM and chat), RedPhone (phone calls), Silent Circle (mobile devices, desktop, and other communications), and Blur and Cocoon (all-in-one privacy extensions for browsing the Internet).

NINJA YOUR IP ADDRESS

Websites and their advertisers are continually logging your unique IP address and tracking what computer you're coming from. This means they have a very good idea of your physical location. If that's something you want to keep private, you should know that you can't trust these businesses (and probably not their employees) with that information. You'll need to decide if this is important for you to put on your privacy list: make a risk assessment about hiding your IP address.

Some people don't mind if their IP address/location is known to websites and their partner businesses. Others find that trying to keep their IP address private is such a pain in the ass that they simply decide to take the risk. Many prefer to only protect their IP address when they're using Wi-Fi or Internet access they don't know or trust. Some people are careful to hide their IP address when they use their laptops in public, like at a café (it helps safeguard against malicious hackers), but they don't bother to hide their IP at home on their own network.

Use Tor

One way to protect your identity as you cruise around the Internet is to use the free *Tor (the onion router)* tool or apps that use Tor, like Orbot for Android. Tor routes your Internet traffic through what's called an *overlay network*, which makes it difficult for nosy people to follow the path your data takes and trace it back to you.

The only problems with Tor are that using it will slow down your Internet traffic and it may not be easy to set up (or troubleshoot) if you're not particularly tech-savvy. Also, if you suddenly start using Tor (or any form of encrypted communications), you may draw the unwanted attention of the authorities, which is of particular concern to female activists. (You'll find a good explanation of how Tor works at *http://eff .org/torchallenge/what-is-tor/.*)

Use a VPN

A significant number of people use a VPN to create a private path for their computers and mobile devices to use when they access the Internet. VPNs are generally easy to use, and there are many to choose from. Your home Internet service provider might even offer one for free. I love how much better I feel using a VPN when I'm at hacker conferences! I can't imagine life without using a VPN, and I can't recommend VPN use strongly enough.

In companies, a VPN is typically used to connect employees who aren't at the workplace to a computer at work; they connect remote employees to central work servers. Many companies have VPNs so workers can access files and other resources over the Internet. Outside of company use, VPNs are being used more and more by people who just want to make their Internet use more secure from attackers.

Most VPNs are encrypted, and that means they'll encrypt your Internet traffic, preventing people from intercepting your connection. Once installed, a VPN is simple to use: just turn it on before you go online (before you open your email, open a browser window, and so on), and you're all set. In a public Wi-Fi environment like a café or airport, you'll need to log in to the Wi-Fi first and then open your VPN before making another move.

To learn more about VPNs, read the article "Why You Should Start Using a VPN (and How to Choose the Best One

for Your Needs)."* When you start your VPN shopping, I recommend reading any recent VPN reviews at Torrent Freak
(*http://torrentfreak.com/*).

Another recommended (and reputable) tool to try is Cocoon.
Cocoon hides your IP address when you access the Internet
with a Cocoon account, and the Cocoon client can be installed
on your browser or on your mobile device.

GET HARD-CORE: MAKE A DATA SILO

In the offline world, a silo is a building where food is stored
in a very secure way. In tech, a data silo is used to store data
files securely to keep them from being accessed, tampered
with, looked at, stolen, or otherwise interfered with.

In regular human life, we can silo certain things from the
rest of our digital world so they don't overlap or get accessed
by apps or companies that do things with our information that
we can't control. Siloed data can't exchange content with other
systems in the organization. The data in a silo remains sealed
off from the rest of the organization, just as grain in a farm silo
is closed off from the outside elements. Grain needs to be closed
off from bugs and germs so it doesn't rot or get contaminated,
and I think of apps and accounts in the same way.

Entities like Facebook, Apple, and Google can creep into
many different apps, sharing our information with them
without us even knowing. One way to prevent this is to rel-
egate them to their own browser: this is a kind of silo. If we
silo Facebook, it can't take our data from other apps without
our consent. If we silo Gmail, critical information in Gmail
doesn't end up in other products or apps unless we want it to.

---

* Alan Henry, "Why You Should Start Using a VPN (and How to Choose the Best One
for Your Needs)," *http://lifehacker.com/5940565/why-you-should-start-using-a-vpn-and-how
-to-choose-the-best-one-for-your-needs/*.

Facebook wants to "infect" all the other apps it can to get more info on me, so I keep it in its own browser (Safari), and I use browser extensions in Firefox that block Facebook's cookies from tracking me when I'm doing my regular news reading and shopping. That way, if I shop at an online vitamin store but decide to quit and leave my shopping cart, I don't get creepy vitamin ads for the things I abandoned in my shopping cart the next time I go to Facebook. I did my shopping only in Firefox and didn't let Facebook spy on me. So when I go to Facebook, it only knows what I choose to share with it.

"I'm always having to be told to brush my hair."
—LENA DUNHAM

10. I hate passwords

Passwords suck. Think about it this way: a password is like a house key, except it's a key that you have to make up yourself without even knowing how the lock works. Plus, you have to remember how to make your key every time you go home.

Because we basically have to invent a new house key every time we password protect an account, lots of us end up using the same key for everything—house, bank, car, school or work locker, hangout spot—which is something you'd never do in real life. Worse, it's a key that any thief can copy using apps they can find on the Internet. So it's no surprise that password cracking is the top way that criminals steal from us.

Unfortunately, we're stuck using password and login credentials for a long time, so if you really want to keep your stuff safe, you'll need to use a bit of password trickery so that when the bad guys come poking around, they'll skip you and go for the person who made his password *123456*.

In this chapter, we'll look at how people steal passwords and then at a few ways you can get all kung fu with your passwords without even breaking a sweat. Just choose the technique that feels right for you, meaning the one that causes you the least stress and annoyance. (Skip to "Password Fu" on page 137 to get right down to business.)

HOW PEOPLE STEAL PASSWORDS

You've probably heard that it's possible to crack passwords with software that you can easily download from the Internet—and this is true. Some programs will run for days or hours, endlessly creating and trying possible passwords for your account (or any account) by attempting to log in with one of these generated passwords. This kind of attack is called brute-forcing; it's kind of like trying thousands of random house keys on a door hoping that one will work. But unlike the door to your house, it's not so easy to try those passwords on a website, because most have safety catches in place to prevent criminals from brute-forcing your accounts.

There are simpler ways to get your password though. One is *shoulder surfing*, where someone watches over your shoulder as you enter your password on your computer or phone while you're logging in on the bus or plane or at a café.

Social engineering is another way that you can have your passwords stolen. Basically, social engineering involves attempts to con you into telling someone your passwords. The person conning you might call you and pretend that they're tech support for Gmail, telling you that you have email stuck somewhere and they need your password to log in and free it up. They might know the names of your friends or colleagues, as well as their phone numbers and email addresses—all of which they can find online via social media sites like LinkedIn, Facebook, Twitter, and people-search sites. Malicious people can also use information they find about you on Facebook and other sites to correctly guess the answers to password-reset questions.

Paris Hilton's phone was attacked using a technique called *inference*. Criminals can use inference to simply guess your passwords based on what they know about you, like your birth date, pet's name, or phone number. The password-reset question for Paris Hilton's phone was her pet's name, which was plastered all over the Internet (and, at the time, on "missing" posters around Beverly Hills).

In another embarrassing example, a well-known hacker had one of his accounts compromised. His password for his Gmail account was "fuckgmail"—and, you guessed it, his other passwords were "fuckamazon," "fuckyahoo," and so on.

You should also know that if you let your Apple device or browser store your passwords in its keychain, then anyone with your computer can read all those passwords. That's why I keep my passwords stored in a strong password manager program (like KeePass, 1Password, or others) instead.

Be wary of websites that ask for your phone number, but in certain situations, like password authentication, giving your phone number to a website is to your advantage. If you can add a phone number to your profile to receive a code to reset (or verify) your password via text message, do it. This is an extra layer of safety for accounts like Gmail, because Creepy Steve can only reset your Gmail password if he also has your phone plus the unlock code to get into your phone in the first place. Nice try, Creepy Steve: you lose.

BUT I HAVE TO SHARE MY PASSWORD

People will tell you over and over that you should never share your passwords, but sometimes you have to. You might need to share a password for a family account, a household account, a photo album you share with someone you love, or a group of friends working on a project.

Here's one thing to know: if a teacher, boss, TSA agent, police officer, or anyone else tells you that you have to give them your password, you shouldn't do it unless you know it's against the law *not* to. Anyone who travels with laptops, phones, and tablets should know what to do if security asks for their password or an agent asks to see what's on their phone and how to protect sensitive or private information if their gadget gets out of their hands.

Egregious digital privacy invasions occur when traveling abroad: US border agents can legally search your laptop or other digital device and copy the contents, as well as confiscate devices. Border agents can do all of this without suspicion or a warrant. And in my opinion, it shouldn't be allowed. Read up on the rules that govern wherever you're traveling to and from before you depart: the EFF maintains a page with more information called "Defending Privacy at the U.S. Border: A Guide for Travelers Carrying Digital Devices."*

However, while traveling inside the US border, it's important to know that the TSA isn't supposed to confiscate laptops, search digital devices, or demand passwords. The TSA's website states, "Should anyone at a TSA checkpoint attempt to confiscate your laptop or gain your passwords or other information, please ask to see a supervisor or screening manager immediately."

In your workplace, check the employee handbook to see what the policy is on passwords; many places state that employees can never share passwords with anyone. If you don't have a handbook, ask your HR manager. If the company rules forbid

---

* Seth Schoen, Marcia Hofmann, and Rowan Reynolds, "Defending Privacy at the U.S. Border: A Guide for Travelers Carrying Digital Devices," *https://www.eff.org/document/ defending-privacy-us-border-guide-travelers-carrying-digital-devices/*.

the sharing of your passwords, yet a boss demands that you provide them, contact HR and email your boss to confirm this request to document it in case anything goes wrong.

If as an employee you have access to anything that would be illegal to share (medical information, banking info, and so on), then you should absolutely contact HR and your company's legal department to notify them of the password-sharing request.

It's illegal for an employer to ask for your personal passwords. In the United States, a federal law was passed in 2013 making it illegal for an employer (or potential employer) to ask for an employee's personal social media passwords. Employers also may not demand that you log in for them (while your boss is standing there) and let them look at your account.

If you share an account with friends or family, do it the smart way. Don't use a password that you use anywhere else. Treat the shared account like any account that can get attacked, but know that its security is weaker than that of an account that you have total control over because it has a shared password. Don't connect that shared account to any other accounts; otherwise an attacker could use that connection to get into those accounts.

Annoy everyone by making them change the shared password regularly, like at least once a month (or more often for even better security).

PASSWORD FU

Search online and you'll find long lists of things to do to help make your passwords stronger and attack-proof. If you decide to use a password manager, these great little apps can generate really strong passwords for you whenever you need one. You can also use password generators on trusted websites, such as LastPass (*http://lastpass.com/generatepassword.php*) or Norton (*http://identitysafe.norton.com/password-generator/*).

Follow these rules and you'll get better passwords:

- Make strong passwords that are at least 12 to 16 characters long.

- Don't use pet or family names.

- Don't use your address, Social Security number, birth date, or other personal information.

- Never recycle or reuse a password—not even once.

- Change your passwords every 10 weeks to 90 days.

- Don't let Chrome, Firefox, Safari, or any other browser save passwords for you.

- Use password phrases (usually six or more words long) for the best security.

- Include capital letters, numbers, and symbols if the app or site allows it.

Once you've created and saved complex passwords for every site, protect them:

- Block shoulder surfing by covering your screen as you enter a password and making sure that no one's observing you.

- Don't tell anyone your password.

- Create passwords that are hard to guess.

- Password protect your phone, tablets, phablets, and computers.

- Use a password manager.

Password managers like LastPass and 1Password save all of your passwords safely in a vault and encrypt everything. That way, you have them all in one place, no one can accidentally discover them, and you can make really complicated passwords, because the manager will keep track of them (and remember them) for you. You use one master password to unlock the password manager, and it saves and encrypts your passwords either locally or on its site. Most of these applications also have crazy-awesome password creators that you can and should use to generate super-strong new passwords with one click—and the password app automatically saves them for you.

Many of these apps can also be set to automatically enter the password for you on websites or into applications during a set time period (after which the password manager shuts down unless you log back in). A lot of security nerds like password managers because the app is the only thing that knows their passwords and they're very secure.

When shopping for a password manager, don't use one that stores your passwords on only one computer, because if your computer gets stolen, then you'll have to reset all of your passwords. This could be really time-consuming, really hard, or impossible. Look for reputable managers like KeePass, oneSafe, 1Password (AgileBits), Password Safe, LastPass, and SplashData. Most of these have both free and paid versions. The free version might be all you need, though the paid versions offer extras such as being fast-tracked for help from a support team or having an ad-free experience.

Before you pick a password manager, make sure it has all the versions you need so that you'll be able to sync passwords on your home computer, tablet, and phone. For instance, LastPass has apps for Apple, Android, Blackberry, Linux, Windows, Safari, Chrome, Opera, Firefox, and Internet Explorer.

"The hardest thing is trying not to correct everything on the Internet. It'd be night and day—wrong, wrong, wrong, wrong. So you just have to say, 'All right, I'll take it, bring it on.'"
—GEORGE CLOONEY

resources

In this chapter, you'll find links to the resources cited in this book. For more supplementary material, visit the book's websites at *http://www.smartprivacy.tumblr.com/* and *http://www.nostarch.com/smartgirlsguide*. I also recommend checking out the Electronic Frontier Foundation (*https://www.eff.org/*), Privacy Rights Clearinghouse (*http://www.privacyrights.org/*), and the Electronic Privacy Information Center (EPIC; *https://www.epic.org/*) for more information on online privacy and your rights.

CHAPTER 1: GET SMART

Google Custom Alerts: *http://google.com/alerts/*

Google Reverse Image search instructions: *https://support.google.com/websearch/answer/1325808?hl=en*

Antitheft Apps (see also Chapter 5)

Lookout: *https://www.lookout.com/*

Prey: *https://preyproject.com/*

Antitracking Plug-ins and Extensions (see also Chapter 8)

AdBlock Plus: *https://adblockplus.org/*

Blur: *https://dnt.abine.com/#register*

Disconnect: *https://disconnect.me/*

Ghostery: *https://www.ghostery.com/en/*

Password Managers (see also Chapter 10)

1Password: *http://www.agilebits.com/onepassword/*

KeePass: *http://www.keepass.info/*

LastPass: *https://lastpass.com/*

Searching Your Name (see also Chapter 7)

Spokeo: *http://www.spokeo.com/*

USSearch*: http://www.ussearch.com/*

Intelius: *http://www.intelius.com/*

CHAPTER 2: BUT IT'S JUST MY PHONE NUMBER

Red Alert List

- Passwords
- Real, full (family) name
- Address of your home, workplace, or school
- Social Security number

- Government ID numbers (driver's license number and passport number)
- Date and place of birth
- Biometric information (fingerprints, facial recognition, voice recognition)
- Computer's IP address (a unique number that identifies your computer on the Internet)
- Specific location (geolocation numbers, like from your phone or in tagged photos)
- Credit and debit card numbers, security codes, and expiration dates
- Bank account numbers
- Answers to common security questions

Yellow Alert List

- Name you use day to day, if different from your legal name
- Primary screen name(s)
- Email address (if it's not public)
- Telephone number
- Race, sexual orientation, and gender
- Mailing address (if it's different from your residence; otherwise it's red)
- Country, state, and city of residence
- ZIP code (or postal code)
- Google Voice number

Green List

- Secondary screen names or account names (say, a throwaway email address that forwards to your primary address)
- Mailing address or PO box
- Digital, online phone number, such as a Skype number
- Email addresses that are not linked to a vital service, such as your bank account
- Photos and videos that don't embarrass you or reveal private information

- Social media profiles on sites where you're confident you understand the privacy settings

- General likes, favorites, and things you enjoy sharing on social media sites

- Single-use or gift credit cards

CHAPTER 3: YOU GOT HACKED

FTC data breach complaint report: *https://www.ftccomplaintassistant .gov/* and click **Identity Theft**

Hack checker: *https://haveibeenpwned.com/* (has many, but not all)

Hard drive recovery: DriveSavers; *http://www.drivesaversdatarecovery .com/*

Account Recovery

Amazon: Use **Help ▶ Contact U**s

AppleCare: *https://www.apple.com/support/applecare/*

eBay: 1.866.961.9253 (Tell them you'd like to talk about "Account—someone has used your account.")

Facebook: *https://www.facebook.com/hacked/*

Google: *http://www.google.com/accounts/recovery/*

Microsoft (Outlook, Xbox, Hotmail, and so on): *https://account.live .com/acsr/*

PayPal: 1.888.221.1161 (Outside the United States, call 1.402.935.2050.)

Twitter: *https://support.twitter.com/forms/hacked/*

Yahoo!: *https://help.yahoo.com/kb/helpcentral/* or 1.800.318.0612

For help finding direct phone numbers that may save you a ton of time, check out *http://gethuman.com/*.

Backup Services and Products

Amazon Cloud Services: *http://aws.amazon.com/backup-recovery/*

Box: *https://www.box.com/personal/file-sync/*

CrashPlan: *http://www.code42.com/crashplan/*

iCloud: *https://www.apple.com/icloud/*

DropBox: *https://www.dropbox.com/*

Create an Account with a New Email Provider

Gmail: *https://accounts.google.com/signup*

Hushmail: *https://www.hushmail.com/signup/*

iCloud: *https://support.apple.com/kb/ph2620?locale=en_US*

Microsoft Outlook: *http://www.microsoft.com/en-us/outlook-com/*
(click **Sign up**)

Yahoo! Mail: *https://overview.mail.yahoo.com/*

Zoho Mail: *https://mail.zoho.com/biz/createAcc.do*

Encryption Products

VeraCrypt: *https://veracrypt.codeplex.com/*

CipherShed: *https://ciphershed.org/*

Encryption Programs

BitLocker for Windows: *https://technet.microsoft.com/en-us/library/cc732774.aspx*

FileVault for Mac: *https://support.apple.com/en-us/HT204837*

Place a Fraud Alert

Equifax: 1.800.525.6285; *http://www.equifax.com/*; PO Box 740241, Atlanta, GA 30374-0241

Experian: 1.888.397.3742; *http://www.experian.com/*; PO Box 2002, Allen, TX 75013

TransUnion: 1.800.680.7289; *http://www.transunion.com/*; Fraud Victim Assistance Division, PO Box 6790, Fullerton, CA 92834-6790

CHAPTER 4: FEMALE TROUBLE

NNEDV (National Network to End Domestic Violence) Technology Safety & Privacy Toolkit for Survivors: Safety tips, information, and privacy strategies for survivors of abuse, stalking, bullying and harassment; *http://techsafety.org/resources-survivors/*

Online copyright infringement claim forms: *http://copyright.gov/onlinesp/agenta.pdf*

Whois lookups: *http://www.whoishostingthis.com/*; *http://www.yougetsignal.com/*

Without My Consent: Legal paths for online harassment victims; *http://www.withoutmyconsent.org/*

Counseling, Therapy, and Support

American Counseling Association: Counselor and therapist locators; *http://www.counseling.org/*

American Psychological Association, Psychology Help Center: *http://www.apa.org/helpcenter/*

Breakthrough.com: Confidential online counseling and therapy

eTherapi.com: Reputable, secure website and network where you can talk to a therapist online

Fight Cyberstalking: *http://www.fightcyberstalking.org/*

National Association of Social Workers: Tips on finding a therapist and resource links; *http://www.helpstartshere.org/find-a-social-worker/*

Rape, Abuse & Incest National Network: Sexual assault and sexual trauma help resources; *https://rainn.org/get-help/* or 1.800.656.HOPE [4673]

Tech savvy therapists who "get it": *http://smartprivacy.tumblr.com/therapists/*

DMCA Takedown Request Services

DMCA Defender: *http://dmcadefender.com/* (Make sure you read reviews or talk to others who have used these services before you trust them with your private problems.)

DMCA email template:

Subject: Copyright Infringement Notification

To <DMCA at WEBSITE NAME>:

1. This document is notification of the copyright infringement of my photos on the website <WWW.WEBSITE.COM>.

2. I am the copyright owner of the photos posted at the following links:

<LINK>
<LINK>

3. I have not assigned or otherwise granted any rights to any third party in the contents now or previously appearing on <WWW .WEBSITE.COM>.

4. I hold exclusive rights to the copyrighted materials infringed.

5. The infringed copyrighted work has been identified in Paragraph 2, and the information has been adequately identified to require that such material be removed or access to it be immediately disabled.

6. I have a good faith belief that the use of the copyrighted material in this manner complained of is not authorized by the law.

7. I swear, under penalty of perjury, that the information of this Notification is accurate and that I am authorized to act on behalf of the owner of an exclusive right that is allegedly infringed.

Please feel free to contact me if you have any questions, and thank you for your time and attention to this matter.

Respectfully,

<YOUR NAME>

<YOUR EMAIL ADDRESS>

Enquiries can be made to:

<LAWYER NAME>

<LAWYER EMAIL, PHONE NUMBER, MAILING ADDRESS>
If it seems this has not reached you, <LAWYER NAME> and their staff will follow up with you in a timely manner for a speedy resolution.

Outsourcing

Amazon's Mechanical Turk: *http://www.mturk.com/*

Elance.com

RemoteStaff.com.au

YourManInIndia.com

Reputation Services and Image Removal

Abine: *https://www.abine.com/*

DMCA Defender: *http://www.dmcadefender.com/*

Reputation.com

Revenge Porn Support Organizations

Army of She: *http://www.armyofshe.com/*

Ban Revenge Porn: *http://www.banrevengeporn.com/*

Crash Override Network: Combating Online Hate: *http://www
.crashoverridenetwork.com*

End Revenge Porn: *http://www.endrevengeporn.org/* and *http://www
.endrevengeporn.org/professionals-helping-victims/*

IWF: *https://www.iwf.org.uk/report/*

Women Against Revenge Porn: *http://www.womenagainstrevengeporn
.com/*

CHAPTER 5: IDENTITY THEFT

Fix credit reports: *http://www.consumer.ftc.gov/articles/0291
-disputing-errors-credit-reporting-companies/*

IRS ID Theft Affidavit Form 14039: *http://www.irs.gov/pub/irs-pdf/
f14039.pdf*

IRS Identity Protection Specialized Unit: 1.800.908.4490

Social Security Administration fraud hotline: 1.800.269.0271

Wipe or overwrite the drive or memory on your phone: Blancco; *http://
dban.org/*

Antitheft Tracking Apps

AVG: *http://www.avg.com/us-en/for-android*

Kapersky: *http://www.kaspersky.com/mobile_security*

Lookout: *https://www.lookout.com/*

McAfee: *http://home.mcafee.com/store?CategoryId=Mobile*

Prey: *https://preyproject.com/*

Where's My Droid: *http://wheresmydroid.com/*

FTC Identity Theft Report

To create: *http://www.consumer.ftc.gov/articles/0277-create-identity-theft-report/*

To file: *http://ftccomplaintassistant.gov/*

Questions: 1.877.IDTHEFT (438.4338)

Place a Fraud Alert and Get Copies of Your Credit Reports

Equifax: 1.800.525.6285

Experian: 1.888.397.3742

TransUnion: 1.800.680.7289

Place a Security Freeze on Your Credit

Equifax: *https://www.freeze.equifax.com/*

Experian: *https://www.experian.com/freeze/center.html*

TransUnion: *http://www.transunion.com/securityfreeze*

CHAPTER 6: HOW TO SHARE

Social Media Privacy Settings

Facebook: *http://www.facebook.com/settings/?tab=privacy/*

Google: *http://www.google.com/dashboard/*; *https://plus.google.com/settings/*; *https://www.google.com/safetycenter/* (for more information on managing and securing your account); *http://myaccount.google.com/*

Twitter: *http://www.twitter.com/settings/security/*

Photo Sharing Site Privacy Settings

Flickr: *https://www.flickr.com/account/privacy/*

Imgur: *https://help.imgur.com/hc/en-us/articles/201746817-Image -and-album-privacy-explained/*

Instagram: *https://help.instagram.com/116024195217477/*

CHAPTER 7: PEOPLE-SEARCH WEBSITES

Find Tracking Companies

Ghostery (*http://www.ghostery.com/*): With their free software download, every time you go to a website, a pop-up window tells you all the companies that are grabbing your data.

PrivacyFix.com: This site tells you only what Google, Yahoo!, BlueKai, Bizo, and eXelate know, but it also lists more than 300 tracking companies and helps you opt out of being tracked by them.

People-Finder Sites

BeenVerified: *http://www.beenverified.com/*

DOBSearch: *https://www.dobsearch.com/*

Intelius: *http://www.intelius.com/*

LexisNexis: *http://www.lexisnexis.com/en-us/products/public -records.page*

Spokeo: *http://www.spokeo.com/*

WhitePages: *http://www.whitepages.com/*

Opt Out of Data Mining

There isn't one single clearinghouse where you can put yourself on a "do not track" list, but you can opt out of data mining by all members of industry associations:

Self-Regulatory Program for Online Behavioral Advertising of the Digital Advertising Alliance (DAA): *http://www.aboutads.info/choices/*

Do Not Track: *http://www.donottrack.us/*

Mobile App Tracking: *http://www.optoutmobile.com/optout/index.html*

Network Advertising Initiative: *http://www.networkadvertising.org/ choices/*

Privacy Rights Clearinghouse has a constantly updated page of people-search information brokers, their removal policies, and links to all removal and opt-out pages (*https://www.privacyrights.org/online -information-brokers-list/*).

The mail template below is one I've used with success on multiple people-search websites via email, fax, and postal mail (first, see if you're listed):

> *Dear <NAME OF COMPANY>:*
>
> *As per your privacy policy, please remove my listing from your databases:*
>
> *a. First name: <YOUR FIRST NAME>*
>
> *b. Last name: <YOUR LAST NAME>*
>
> *c. Middle initial: <YOUR MIDDLE INITIAL>*
>
> *d. Aliases & AKAs: <ANY ALIASES OR OTHER NAMES, MAIDEN NAME, ETC.>*
>
> *e. Current address: <YOUR ADDRESS>*
>
> *f. Age: <YOUR AGE>*
>
> *g. DOB: <YOUR DATE OF BIRTH>*
>
> *Thank you for your assistance.*

CHAPTER 8: DATING AND SEXYTIME

Sample in-person safety guidelines for online dating: *http://www .chemistry.com/help/safety/*

Browser Plug-ins and Extensions

Adblock Plus: Blocks ads and tracking for most advertisers; *https:// adblockplus.org/.*

AppLock: *https://play.google.com/store/apps/details?id=com.domobile .applock*

AVG PrivacyFix: Manages all social media privacy settings; *https:// www.privacyfix.com/start/install.*

Blur: Blocks tracking, password management, disposable email addresses, and much more; *https://dnt.abine.com/#register.*

BugMeNot: Bypasses the sign-in on websites that require your info to simply read a page; *http://bugmenot.com/.*

Cocoon: Blocks tracking, offers disposable email addresses; *https://getcocoon.com/*.

Disconnect: Blocks Facebook tracking; *https://disconnect.me/*.

Do Not Track: *http://donottrack.us/*

DuckDuckGo: A nontracking search engine; *https://duckduckgo.com/*

Ghostery: Alerts you to bugs, tracking, and ad networks on sites you visit but can be overwhelming and controversially resells anonymized user metrics; *https://www.ghostery.com/en/*.

HTTPS Everywhere: Enables encryption automatically on sites that support it; *https://www.eff.org/HTTPS-EVERYWHERE*.

PrivacySuite: *https://addons.mozilla.org/en-US/firefox/addon/privacysuite/*

Privoxy: Ad blocker and web proxy for more technical users to customize fine-grained browser security; *http://www.privoxy.org/*

Browser Security Settings

Chrome: **Settings** ▸ (Show advanced settings) **Privacy**

Firefox: **Preferences** ▸ **Privacy**

Internet Explorer: **Tools** ▸ **Internet Options** ▸ **Privacy**

Safari: **Preferences** ▸ **Privacy** (and **Preferences** ▸ **Security**)

Safari mobile: **Settings** ▸ **Safari** ▸ **Privacy & Security**

CHAPTER 9: NINJA TRICKS

Find your current IP address: *http://www.whatismyip.com/*

PO box application: *https://poboxes.usps.com/poboxonline/search/landingPage.do*

VPN, reliable reviews: *http://www.torrentfreak.com/?s=VPN/*

Credit Freezes and Fraud Alerts

Experian: *http://experian.com/freeze/center.html*; *http://experian.com/fraud/center.html*

TransUnion: *http://transunion.com/securityfreeze/*; *http://fraud*
.transunion.com/

Equifax: *https://www.freeze.equifax.com/*; *https://www.alerts*
.equifax.com/

Prepaid Credit Cards/Gift Cards

Amex: *http://www.americanexpress.com/gift-cards/*

Discover: *http://www.discover.com/gift-cards/index.shtml*

MasterCard: *http://www.mastercard.us/prepaid-gift-card.html*

Visa: *http://usa.visa.com/personal/personal-cards/gift-cards/*

Masked cards (unique, disposable credit cards): MaskMe; *http://www*
.abine.com/maskme/

OpenPGP Encryption

How it works: *http://www.explainthatstuff.com/encryption.html*;
Cryptography.org; "PGP Installation and Use For Dummies," *http://*
www.qdog.com/pgp/pgp_faq.html

Browser extension: Mailvelope; *https://www.mailvelope.com/*

Open source alternative: *https://www.gnupg.org/*

OTR

How it works: *http://www.pressfreedomfoundation.org/encryption*
-works#otr, otr.cypherpunks.ca

Chat/IM software clients that come with OTR: Adium, *https://*
adium.im/; Xabber, *http://www.xabber.com/*; TextSecure, *https://*
whispersystems.org/; ChatSecure, *https://chatsecure.org/*

Chat/IM software client that supports OTR plug-ins: Pidgin; *https://*
pidgin.im/

Recommended Privacy Apps

Blur: *https://www.abine.com/index.html*

ChatSecure: *https://chatsecure.org/*

Cocoon: *https://getcocoon.com/*

RedPhone and Text Secure: *https://whispersystems.org/*

Silent Circle: *https://www.silentcircle.com/* and *https://blackphone.ch/*

Tor (The Onion Router)

Project site: *https://www.torproject.org/*

How it works: *https://www.eff.org/torchallenge/what-is-tor/*

Apps that use Tor: Orbot for Android; *https://guardianproject.info/apps/orbot/*

VoIP

BurnerApp: *http://www.burnerapp.com/*

Google Voice: *https://www.google.com/googlevoice/about.html*

Skype: *http://www.skype.com/en/*

CHAPTER 10: I HATE PASSWORDS

Password Generators

LastPass: *http://lastpass.com/generatepassword.php*

Norton: *http://identitysafe.norton.com/password-generator/*

Password Managers

1Password: *http://www.agilebits.com/onepassword/*

KeePass: *http://www.keepass.info/*

LastPass: *https://lastpass.com/*

oneSafe: *http://www.onesafe-apps.com/*

Password Safe: *http://www.passwordsafe.sourceforge.net/*

Splash ID Safe: *http://www.splashdata.com/*

index